5   6   7

D0992450

110°   120° (KHINGAN MTS.)

A

Residence of
Hsiung Nu chief

N U   (GOBI
DESERT)

W U · H U A N

Great Wall   Liaotung
Hsüant'u

Liaohsi   C H' A O · H S I E N

B

hüyen   Yünchung   Shangku
Kaoch'üeh   Yenmen   Yen   Lolang
Wuyüan   Tinghsiang

P o h a i   S e a

II   Shuofang   T'aiyüan   P'ingyüan   Tzuch'uan
wei   Ch'angshan   Chinan   Lintzu
Ho   Hantan   + MT. T'AI   Ch'üfu
Chinch'eng   P'ingyang   Honei   Ch'enliu   P'eng

Lunghsi   Ch'angan   Loyang   Yingch'üan
Wei   Nanyang   Huai   Kuangling

Hanchung   Han   Huainan   Wu
Yüan

Chiang   Kueichi

Shu   Nan   Chiang   Hofei   (Yangtze)
Pa   Yüchang

Ch'angsha

Eastern
Sea

C

D

N O N - C H I N E S E   T R I B E S   M I N   Y Ü E H

T I E N   Ichou

(Hsi)   N A N   Y Ü E H   P'anyü

Chiaochih

Southern
Sea

E

5   6   7   8

CHINA:
An Interpretive History

CHINA:
AN INTERPRETIVE
HISTORY

From the Beginnings
to the Fall of Han

Joseph R. Levenson
and
Franz Schurmann

University of California Press

BERKELEY, LOS ANGELES, LONDON

University of California Press
Berkeley and Los Angeles, California
University of California Press, Ltd.
London, England
Copyright © 1969 by the Regents of the University of California
Second printing, 1971
First paperbound edition, 1971
International Standard Book Number 0-520-01440-5 (clothbound edition)
0-520-01892-3 (paperbound edition)
Library of Congress Catalog Card Number: 75-78566
Printed in the United States of America

In Memory of a Friend

On April 6, 1969, my friend Joe Levenson drowned in the Russian River of Northern California.

When a friend is alive, we see him only in his parts. Only when he is gone forever, do these parts come together in the unity of a full man. In reading the proofs of this book which bears Joe's imprint throughout, I sensed for the first time the nature of his quest. The history of China was an analogy to his own life, as a human being, as an intellectual, as a giver of love and friendship to many others, as a believing Jew, as a man who valued beauty and community. What he saw in China was not change with continuity, but fierce diversity which again and again reconstituted itself into unity. For Joe, China was not the triumph of Confucianism as it has been conventionally seen in the field. Nor was China the resultant institutionalization of forces, as it has appeared to me. He saw Confucianism, the doctrines of authoritarian social responsibility, as sharply opposed to the self-oriented anarchism of Taoism. These creeds and the men who upheld them did not live harmoniously together over the many centuries of Chinese history. They fought each other, sometimes bloodily. Yet somehow out of these conflicts came the spirit of syncretism. Confucianism and Taoism, and the many other conflicting currents in China, did not compromise with each other, nor did they learn to live together in peace. What made syncretism possible was the consciousness, learning, and above all humankindness of the Chinese. They realized, already in antiquity, that man has many needs, many parts. If one part overrides or is stunted, then the dialectic of *yin* and *yang* will change the constellation of forces, sometimes peacefully, sometimes violently. But the invisible hand of harmony always operates.

Joe began his life of thought on China with questions on the decline of Confucianism, and the substitution for it of revolutionary creeds. Then he looked at contemporary China, seeing there the reappearance of diversity ("regionalism"). When we conceived this volume on China's history, we injected into the material of history the problems of our own lives we each wrestled with. Our problems differed, yet the country and history of China are so rich that there were analogies enough for all. The spirit of syncretism preoccupied Joe more and more, as is reflected in this volume.

Like the rich country and history of China, Joe was a human being of many parts. In his life and thought, with more struggle than many of us recognized, he began to realize a syncretism. Perhaps as these volumes were coming into being, the syncretism of his own life and thought would too have developed.

Alone now, I only can offer this volume to the readers. But if we read what Joe has written over the years, we may be able to finish in thought what he has not been able to do in life.

Franz Schurmann
May, 1969

Preface

What should China mean in a history curriculum for western students? Once upon a time it may have seemed that knowledge of China had its value because it was explicitly outside the student's main concern; this is the value of an exotic fillip. More recently, and plausibly, the emphasis has shifted to China as a major area in world affairs — what one seeks is knowledge of an area that is politically important to the fate of western peoples.

These two points of view seem quite different. Yet, both of them are solipsistic, both of them measure the value of Chinese studies by how they embroider a western culture or how they contribute to western political survival. The intrinsic intellectual interest of this history tends to be overlooked. But China, ancient and modern, is more than exotic, and China is more than a political factor that we need to take into account (though it is that, too); it is an area whose history raises questions of the broadest intellectual concern. If we really mean what we all say now about our discovery of the full dimensions of the modern world, our moral and intellectual realization that European and American histories are not the whole story, we will study Chinese history for its universal significance, not just for its relevance to the needs, political or cultural, of our part of the world.

We have written this book, then, in the conviction that Chinese history is neither an intellectual frill for the western student, nor a discipline simply forced on the good citizen by what he may feel to be the distastefully growing complexity of the modern world. Instead it is really, organically, involved in modern knowledge. Chinese material belongs in the truly universal world of the understanding, transcending area boundaries.

Hoping to bring this out, we have written a book perhaps unconventional as a history text. The chronological principle has been maintained — history has to be, after all, a study of process in unilinear time. However, with our emphasis on the intellectual content of the study rather than on "area" accumulation, we have tried to make the process of learning a process of deepening sophistication, not just a lengthening catalogue of data as time and pages go by. The book is not spun out on the principle of another day, another dynasty. The dynasties come, but new material is not just tacked on to the raw end; rather, as the arc of time lengthens, the old material is constantly reinvoked, as more complex, overarching problems are formulated. In effect, as far as the chronologically accumulating data are concerned, the student's notes are taken for him, in the first section of each chapter. In the second section, assuming the data and emerging out of them, are those definitions of intellectual problems that are at least some of the ends of study, but that so often struggle vainly to be born in the minds of students diverted wholly to means. These problems might be the core of a course, and through them an instructor who is not a specialist in Chinese studies may yet make his training in his own special field really relevant here (instead of irrelevant to a need felt to "work up" the area data). He really has something to add — the maturity of the guide — instead of just feeling dependent on the same aggregation of foreign detail as he may be assigning his students. And Chinese specialists, too, may welcome a presentation of their subject as a contrapuntal series of problems, which may convert students from passive listeners to questing, creative users of their instructor's expertise.

Acknowledgments
We wish to acknowledge with thanks permission from
Mr. M. B. Yeats, the Macmillan Companies of Canada and London, and Macmillan & Co., Inc., New York, to quote on p. 52 from "The Scholars" in *The Collected Poems of W. B. Yeats* (1959);
George Allen & Unwin Ltd., London, to quote on p. 52 from *The Book of Songs*, trans. by Arthur Waley (1937);
Harvard University Press, Cambridge, Mass., to quote on p. 52 from Ezra Pound, *The Classic Anthology by Confucius* (1954);
Alfred A Knopf, Inc., New York, to quote on p. 114 from *Chinese Poems* trans. by Arthur Waley (1964).

Contents

ix

Prelude

Background

"Peking Man"
(Homo Erectus Pekinensis)

Beginning summer, 1926, with the discovery of two human teeth in a cave in Hopei province, thirty-seven miles southwest of Peking, a series of finds through 1929 in related sites established the existence of palaeolithic (old stone age) man in China, about 400,000 years ago. Bones (including a complete cranium), fossilized animal remains, and crude stone tools of an unstandardized or occasional type were found together. (Palaeolithic tools, though no human remains, had been found in 1920.) Analogies have been seen with Mousterian and Aurignacian palaeolithic remains in Europe, dating from the latter part of the Pleistocene or Ice Age.

On the evolutionary scale, "Peking man" comes later than Pithecanthropus erectus ("Java man") and earlier than Neanderthal.

This bit of information begins Chinese history with what seems easy and indisputable: the beginning. But this topic and the next one raise a difficult question. Here, in *Background*, we record an undoubted fact about the past, something literally true. Is it unequivocally "history"? In *Background* of Chapter 1, dealing with legends, we shall record some nonfacts, things literally false. Are they unequivocally "nonhistory"? In our discussion in *Implications*, and subse-

1

quently, we suggest that a mode of thought, the historical point of view, must intrude on the data to settle the question. History is neither just a receptacle for "fact" nor a repeller of "fantasy."

Reading

Fairservis, Walter A., Jr., *The Origins of Oriental Civilization* (New York: Mentor Books, 1959). Paperback.

Implications

History and Cultural Continuity

Before people ever lived, geological processes were working themselves out in time. Was this history? What gives it an air of history, if anything does, is the fact that people finally arrived on the geological scene, with their lives conditioned by what had happened in geological time. At some point, culture must impinge upon landscape, "the earth" become "the world," if human beings (the only ones who have the historical mode of knowledge) are to qualify passing time as "historical".

But do people in the abstract have a history as merely universal people, with individual cultures still undifferentiated? If a sense of cultural continuity is indispensable to the historical appreciation, then "prehistoric man" is rightly named; without such things as an aesthetic and a script, style and stylus — precisely the sort of cultural achievement that sets one people off from another (as Chinese, for example) — no continuity can be traced, and man has no more history than the animals from which he derives. Biological evolution is just that — biological — not historical, and there is nothing about "Peking man" in himself to make him a figure in Chinese history. He is just man in the abstract at an evolutionary stage, with no visible ties of particular cultural continuity down through time to the Chinese people, one of those differentiated groups of humans that alone can have a history.

And yet, like the moon which has no light of its own but nevertheless shines with the borrowed light of the sun, "Peking man" is given a historical character by the historical retrospect of culturally differentiated men. The very name, "Peking man," conveys its sense of location only because true history eventually happened there and in the larger China which Peking inescapably suggests. The very ideas, "Peking," "China," would be unthinkable if history had not intervened. Without it (and at the time of "Peking man" himself the world was still without it), these primitive human remains would belong to just a nondescript bit of geological crust.

By naming him "Peking man," modern historical man *creates* him as a historical figure. Objectively speaking, "Peking man" does not begin Chinese history; it is only because Chinese history ultimately (long after) really does begin that he comes to be placed at its beginning. That is why, when in the 1920's one Western interpretation of the palaeontological evidence suggested that "Peking man" was a cannibal (and probably within his own family circle), some Chinese, consciously imbued with historical Chinese culture, with its humanism and its emphasis on family solidarity, were shocked and resentful. "Peking man" did nothing we will ever know to set a specifically Chinese history in motion. Rather, it was *that history* which imposed a historical status on "Peking man," by placing him in a space that only history stamped as "China," and by suggesting, therefore, that continuity somehow must exist.

Background

Chinese Origins: The Legends

By the fourth century A.D., the Chinese succession of mythic creative figures was completely formulated, as follows (in main lines):

P'an Ku (shaper of the universe: never near the center of Chinese political or religious ideas. His myth was non-Chinese in origin.)

The "Three August Ones" (Fu Hsi, Shen Nung, Huang Ti or the "Yellow Emperor"), (associated respectively with hunting, agriculture, and the establishing of family names).

The "Five Rulers" (the last two being Yao and Shun).

Yü (founder of the Hsia dynasty, first of the "three eras" that became for later generations the Classical Period).

An eighteenth-century Chinese scholar (who did not himself make cross-cultural comparisons) established these figures as illustrations of what seems almost a law of folklore: the later the story teller, the more readily he will supply detail about an earlier and earlier past. Thus, ostensibly the earliest figure in this catalogue, P'an Ku, emerges latest in the literature (fourth century A.D.); the "Three August Ones," later in the legendary chronology, appear earlier in the texts, in the Later Han period (23–220 A.D.); Ssu-ma Ch'ien (145–90? B.C.), earlier still, knows only the "Five Rulers" in his *Shih-chi* (*Records of the Historian*); while the

4

earliest text of all, the Classic known as *Shu-ching* (*Book of Documents*, its basic stratum being of the Chou period, ca. 1000–221 B.C.), has only the latest three of the legendary sage-kings, Yao, Shun, and Yü.

Some legends:

There are Chinese versions of the almost ubiquitous story of the great deluge. In one of them, the "Yellow Emperor" (Huang Ti, last of the "Three August Ones"), sent down his daughter, Pa, to stop the flood. She was, as it were, a goddess of dryness, and plants and animals died everywhere she went. The "Yellow Emperor," to repair the damage, carried Pa north of the Red Waters, which separated the inhabited world from the desert. Then the "Yellow Emperor" sowed the ground again, and men were taught to work the fields.

In a more prominent legend, the flood was conquered by Yü, who pierced gaps in the mountains for drainage. "But for Yü we should all have been fishes."

Yao and Shun (who immediately preceded Yü in the great trinity of sage-kings), were particularly famous, Yao for appointing a successor of different family name (i.e., for sageliness, not lineage), Shun for inventing the writing brush.

Reading

Bodde, Derk: Myths of Ancient China: in Kramer, Samuel N. (ed.), *Mythologies of the Ancient World* (New York: Doubleday Anchor Books, 1961).

Implications

The Relation of "Legend" to "Fact"

When men first become aware of themselves as a cultural community, they formulate ideas of the past, to explain how they became what they are. What relation have their ideas of the past to the ideas of modern outsiders? Is it enough to say that the legend makers could only guess, or repeat the fancies of their naturally naïve ancestors, while our modern scientific techniques of inquiry bring us nearer "the facts"?

If we answer the question affirmatively, we make the question unnecessarily one of alternatives, as much as to say that both sets of ideas are merely rival explanations of the same body of mute data.

But, however untrue to history the legends may be as secondary sources for the story of Chinese origins, they are eminently historical as primary sources for the cultural ideals of the men who wrote them down. And modern historians, precisely through their appreciation of what the legends tell us about their later Chinese redactors, themselves explore the earlier history as the problem of social and intellectual development down to just the type of man who would (and did) write *these* legends into traditional Chinese histories. We have suggested that the men who took the legends as their versions of the past meant to explain how they became what they were. But what were they? — *not* just men, but men with a particular cultural point of view. Naturally, in their legends, they projected their own ideals back into history, so that now we may look into history for the causes of the emergence of these all-pervasive ideals. We cannot believe things happened as the legends literally say. But what the legends mean is that the ancient past was of a certain character, such a character that men who came at the end of it described it in just this (to us) unacceptable way. We must ask why these men should have done so. Historical knowledge never proceeds out of mere exposure to raw data. The latter need questions asked of them, the right questions. The Chinese origin legends, far from being irrelevant to modern inquiry, vividly raise the question that must be at its heart.

The modern historian, then, knows that to account ultimately for the appearance and acceptance of such a seminal work as the *Shih-chi* (*Records of the Historian*) of Ssu-ma Ch'ien, which in the dawn stage of imperial China (Former Han period, 206 B.C.–9 A.D.) gave classical form to many of the stories of antiquity, he has the epic of the taming of the

North China wilderness to deal with, and the establishment of the sedentary agricultural life as the characteristic setting of traditional Chinese civilization; he sees the control and supply of water as an established major concern of sophisticated government, and hostility between the desert and the sown as a fixed motif of Chinese civilization; he is challenged by the rise of literary virtues to preeminence and the socially remarkable disposition to take "virtue," not birth, as giving title to political authority. The sage-kings of the legends are nothing less than symbols of the most typical activities and cherished values of Chinese civilization. Why they became typical, why they became cherished are questions that the moderns ask; and, as literal accounts of the ancient past, modern works have superseded the traditional narratives. But the latter have given the former their proper subject, and thus have been rather absorbed than displaced by the complex newer history.

Background

Prehistory and the Emergence
of Shang

PREHISTORIC CULTURES

Neolithic sites (i.e., areas of human settlement in the "New Stone Age," ending ca. 2000 B.C.) have now been discovered in almost all major areas of China. There are sites in Manchuria, in the Central Plain, in Kansu and farther to the northwest, in the Yangtze Plain, and in the extreme south, Kwangtung, and even in Hong Kong. Objects that have been recovered from these sites show evidence of settled villages, agriculture, domestication of animals, and a certain amount of economic exchange. Cowrie shells, for example, have been found in remote regions of the interior, indicating some trade relationship with the coastal regions of the Pacific.

The "pottery" types

There are certain culture types that seem to have prevailed over large areas, though never over China as a whole. First, there is the "painted pottery" culture type *Yang-shao*, named after its first excavation site, in Honan. There is another type — called *Lung-shan*, after the Shantung site near the place of its discovery — that is characterized by black pottery. In the central and southern regions of China types other than these two have been found. The *Yang-shao* culture has some claim to be regarded as the primary neolithic culture of northern China. *Yang-shao* remains have been found in Honan, Shensi, Shansi, and some areas farther west, in precisely those regions that the legends suggest as the homeland of Chinese civilization.

One of the most interesting facts about *Yang-shao* culture is its apparent affinity with cultures far to the west, in particular those of the lower Volga (the Tripol'e site). There is a tradition in Chinese legends that the Hsia people, the putative predecessors of Shang, came into China from the west. Many modern Chinese scholars, too, believe that the ancestors of the Chinese, the pre-Shang people, migrated into north China from a western region. Recent Soviet archaeological research on the Siberian neolithic era points to racial and cultural connections stretching almost across Siberia, from the Urals to the reaches of Mongolia. This parallel suggests that something may have linked the people of Yang-shao with peoples farther west — perhaps trade, or some common development — but the ties were undoubtedly not as close as certain nineteenth-century writers (like the fantasist Terrien de la Couperie) imagined. Whatever the intimations of affinities between East and West, there is still no hard evidence of diffusion.

Of a different type was the *Lung-shan* culture of black pottery and oracle bones. Sites were found first in the eastern reaches of China, in Shantung, Liaoning, and parts of south Manchuria. It was widely assumed that *Yang-shao* and *Lung-shan* were mutually exclusive contemporaneous cultures. But excavations in the 1950's showed proto-*Lung-shan* cultural elements in strata above *Yang-shao* remains in Honan, Shansi, and Shensi. The most acceptable hypothesis now has the *Yang-shao* and *Lung-shan* cultures not so much distributed in space as developmental in time: the latter evolving from the former, not colliding with it. This culture radiated from the Honan heartland, and became diversified. One of the varieties, close to home (in a Honan-Anhwei-Shantung contiguous area), became the civilization of Shang.

The sites of central and southern China — least studied of Chinese neolithic sites — show greatest affinities with areas farther south, in regions of the Pacific. We know that well into historic times, central and southern China was settled by non-Chinese peoples, remnants of which remain today in China. Though proto-*Lungshan* village farmers penetrated the region in neolithic times, South China as a predominantly "Chinese" area is the product of later colonization.

SHANG

In the first millenium B.C., when Chinese historiographers projected onto the past the conceptions and images of their own times, the Shang or Yin was regarded as China's second dynasty, following the Hsia. The Hsia dynasty, according to the legends, had been founded by the Emperor Yü, the successor of the "Five Rulers" who established Chinese civilization. We may speak of the immediately pre-Shang people as Hsia, but hard archaeological evidence (as distinct from legend) of an organized cultural and political order begins with Shang. Though there are many neolithic sites, the bronze age site at An-yang (in the bend of the Yellow River, in modern Honan), location of the great city of the Shang, is the oldest site in which Chinese writing has been found. And since we have no evidence of large political units in neolithic China, or of formalized class distinction, aristocracy, and a degree of political unity, imposed from the central city, seem to come with Shang, the founder of Chinese civilization — if civilization be what its name implies, the culture of cities (*civitates*).

We cannot say with certainty how the first real city arose in China. However, something may be gleaned of the processes leading to this important event. The North China plain, during the neolithic age, was apparently dotted with numerous agricultural settlements, some of which had already begun to develop a high division of labor. The discovery of pottery and metallic objects indicates that some form of handicraft, perhaps organized handicraft, existed at that time. There may have been an agricultural surplus, favored by the natural fertility of north China's loess soil. Although north China was undoubtedly more thickly forested than it is today, in other respects north China must already have been an open plain distinctly vulnerable to incursions from the northwest and the northeast. Along with agriculture and its predecessors, hunting and fishing, some form of pastoralism also existed and played an important part in the economy.

Permanent village settlements, attendant upon the advancement of agriculture, evolved into petty urban agglomerations and local states. Conflicts ensued. In the course of these conflicts, and following them, the "Shang" people (named for their last capital, on the site of the modern Anyang) achieved the complex political organization that we know as the Shang (or Yin) dynasty. The Shang dynasty is said to have begun in 1766 B.C.; this traditional date is unrealistically precise, but the earliest dynastic sites do appear to date from about the middle of the eighteenth century B.C. Legend traces the Shang to a remote ancestor named Hsieh, said to be the son of one of the "Five Heavenly Emperors," K'u. K'u gave his son, Hsieh, a fief in the Shang district of what is now Shensi Province, whence the name Shang for the dynasty. But the name seems to be genuine, for it is recorded in the oracle bones as the name of their capital.

What are the "oracle bones"? Archaeological evidence for the historical existence of Shang began to appear in the Anyang area in 1899, when curious bone fragments, then being used in the preparation of powdered medicines, came to the attention of scholars and collectors. These fragments, and similar finds from the formal excavations that followed, have been identified as tortoise shells and ox and sheep scapulas, many of them inscribed with the earliest extant versions of Chinese characters. (Some of the latter were also found, subsequently, on scattered bronzes, jades, and pottery vessels.) The shell and bone inscriptions were used exclusively in the divination services of Shang kings. The object was heated in a prepared hollow on one side, so that a pattern of cracks on the other side, the inscribed side, would give the omen.

Reading

Chang Kwang-chih, *The Archaeology of Ancient China* (New Haven: Yale University Press, 1968).

Implications

The Historical Point of
Departure—to What?

We have made two shots at a beginning for Chinese history. Now there should be an unequivocal beginning, with Shang — unequivocal because we have primary sources (archaeological, not literary in the usual sense). Yet, there are still relativities to consider. What did Shang mean to Confucian historical thinkers, to post-Confucianists of the twentieth century, and to Chinese Communists in particular?

We have seen that the Chinese creators and transmitters of the origin legends constructed a far-off past not only out of dim remembrances but out of their own living ideals — the achievements of the legendary heroes could be construed as leading out of the shadows to just those features of life and thought that seemed truly significant in the full light of actual history. When we move into that history, the archaeologically verifiable Shang era, we moderns, like the classical Chinese, tend to bind this segment of the past to what seems most significant in later history. This is what it means to take Shang as the point of departure for *Chinese* history. The limiting adjective, "Chinese," implies that at last we see (not just imaginatively project) the thread of continuity, so that changes in time are not merely a baffling flux: an entity persists in which we can discern the changes operating. When we assume that Shang is truly Chinese we are assuming that the entity is there, and that Shang will never be irrelevant to whatever we single out as significant in later periods of a changing China.

In Confucian historiography Shang is relevant because of a political assumption about its rise and fall. If Hsia (still "legendary" to the moderns) was founded by the sage-king Yü, Hsia was finished by the evil king Chieh, who yielded to the Shang founder, the sage-king T'ang. And the Shang dynasty then went the way of Hsia, with a final royal monster ("He has ripped up pregnant women": one of the milder charges) and an evil-to-virtue handing over to Chou. That is, Shang, in this conception, exemplifies for the first time the full cycle from dynastic succession to dynastic succession (for only Shang, not its dynastic predecessor, Hsia, arose from antecedent moral corruption and breakdown). To Confucianists, political to the core (as we shall see), their ideal sphere of action being the state and their ethics being fundamentally tied to the governing of men, Shang as *political prototype* was perfectly appropriate.

A modern non-Confucian or post-Confucian interpretation takes note of such a political emphasis as a long-persisting feature of Chinese culture and, consistent with this inclusive interest in culture — of which politics are only a part — looks to Shang as a *cultural source*. Of the first importance for cultural continuity are the Shang specimens, on ritual bronzes and "oracle bones," of what is recognizably, despite all later permutations, the Chinese written character. But Shang not only began the continuity of Chinese culture with this incalculably important tool of written language; Shang began its expansion, north and south, from the Yellow River valley region around An-yang (the site of the earliest language evidence, in modern Honan). It was the culture of the Shang people that was carried far afield and, with local accretions, became Chinese culture. Or, we should say, assimilation to the culture whose central line went back to Shang became the traditional historic criterion of "Chineseness." Just as Greek ("Hellenic") education, not Greek ethnic individuality, formed the "Hellenistic" culture of the post-Alexandrian Mediterranean littoral, so a Chinese civilization, not a Chinese ethnic character, became the prime Chinese historical concern, and people who were originally non-Chinese could be thought of as *not yet* Chinese, ultimately to become Chinese.

Nothing so stamped the Shang dynasty's life as the manner of its leaving it. We have suggested that the Confucian tradition's legends about high antiquity relate to modern historiography by making the moderns aware of the development to just this legend-making as the development that moderns must explain. Similarly, the traditional, exclusively political-moralist Confucian emphasis on the evil and virtue of rulers in the Shang-Chou transition, by its very avoidance of any ethnic issue, testifies to the early acceptance (which was to be lasting) of cultural assimilation as sufficient to bring foreign peoples (in this first instance, non-Shang peoples) into a validly Chinese world. If it is sufficient to see the succession from "bad" late Shang to "good" early Chou as a perfectly proper and sufficient continuity, then the original "foreignness" of the Chou (confirmed culturally by such original distinctions as Chou burial in mounds as against Shang burial in flat-topped graves, and Chou abandonment of the Shang practice of human sacrifice) could be accommodated to Chinese canons of legitimacy. In this way, too — as in matters of script and casting of bronze vessels (though Chou used greater elaboration, raising Shang ornamentation in relief, and so on) — the Chou succession established Shang as the primary bearers of Chinese culture; for the "culturalism" of Shang carried down in time, and ethnically foreign conquest peoples could always aspire to be (until a strictly modern *nationalism* supervened) legitimately "Chinese," as the Chou tribes, conquerors from the west, emerged Chinese from the Shang matrix.

Yet, though the distinction between Shang and Chou was not a distinction between two nations, something perceptible as a class distinction can be traced back to the Chou conquest of Shang. A fairly late poem in the Chou collection, the *Book of Songs* (or *Odes*, or *Poetry*), the *Shih-ching*, sounds like Shang *versus* Chou, in the form of peasant protest of "men of the East" against aristocratic luxuriants, "men of the West." One has only to recall the Germanic and Viking conquests in post-Roman Europe, with their enormous contribution to the making of nobilities, to see the Chou conquest of Shang in relation to the Chinese feudal age that followed — *Chinese* still, as Shang must be called Chinese, but feudal, and relatively novel in that social respect. It was not the only way to produce aristocrats; Shang had them and the later Roman empire in the West. But nothing exacerbates class distinctions like a foreign-conquest factor in stratification.

We shall soon turn to the problem of feudalism and its implications for the future. For now, it is enough to discuss its implications for interpretations of the past, the era that lay behind the Chou. The most general Marxist interpretation of history, which became known in Chinese intellectual circles in the 1920's and predominant in the 1950's, assumes a regular succession of social ages: feudalism is taken to be the third of these, preceded in order by (a) "primitive communism" and (b) "slave society," the first "class" society. From this point of view, it is as a slave society that Shang is fixed in the line of Chinese continuity. If, as the weight of non-Confucian opinion has it, pre-Shang is pre-history, that will do nicely for "primitive," and Shang, everywhere accepted as an organized society with signs of division of labor, becomes available for the "slave" characterization.

The evidence is inconclusive. It depends mainly on the interpretation of characters on "oracle bones," that is, the character *fa* 伐, meaning "kill," "cut down." This is used clearly in the sense of "sacrifice." Sometimes there is no context of "captives." Then were the victims slaves? And what of *chung* 眾, a character found in the oldest, early Chou stratum of the *Book of Documents* (*Shu-ching*), in a section dealing with a mid-Shang king. *Chung* designates what may be called, vaguely, "the masses." Were they in some sense slaves? That is what a Marxist scholar, Kuo Mo-jo, concluded in an influential study published in 1945.

Actually, the existence of slaves in a society is not in itself sufficient from the Marxist point of view to define a "slave society," one in which material production rests, on the whole, on slave labor. The Marxist construction of Shang history seems rather a leap of faith than an inevitable conclusion from sufficient evidence. There is not simply belief, but a will to believe. The reasons for it, the secret of the wide appeal of this answer to the Shang problem, are profoundly embedded in modern history. For, just as ancient legends about the still more ancient past are clues to the character of the society that chose to believe them, so a modern image of Shang antiquity may tell us more about the eye of the Marxist beholder than about the facts of the past beheld.

Background

Shang Society

When the Shang (Yin) people first entered the stage of history, they were most likely a tribal people, knowing agriculture but still practicing hunting and fishing, and already acquainted with the domestication of animals. When the Shang dynasty ended, the Shang people had become the aristocratic rulers of a considerable domain in north China, controlled from a great city — the city of Shang, unearthed in the modern excavations at An-yang — which became their permanent capital. The classical Chinese sources speak repeatedly of "movements of the capital": from the time of Hsieh, the legendary primeval ancestor of the Shang people, to T'ang, the reputed founder of the Shang dynasty, the capital is supposed to have been moved eight times. From T'ang to P'an Keng, five such movements are recorded. The fifth, to the An-yang site, marked the last and definitive movement of the Shang people.

The references to "movements of the capital" have suggested to some writers that the Shang may have been nomadic. It is true that among the later nomads of Inner and Central Asia, there were often no fixed "capitals," the "capital" moving along with the tribe. However, even after the nomads had succeeded in conquering a sedentary society, they still maintained the habit of shifting their capitals periodically; and when they no longer shifted their capitals they changed residence according to seasons, moving to highlands in the summer and back to the lowlands in the winter. Before the establishment of Nara (710 A.D.) the Japanese emperors also shifted capitals periodically, usually after the death of an emperor. It is unlikely that the Shang people were nomads in the sense of the later Turks and Mongols, for large-scale steppe nomadism probably arose with the domestication of the horse, which occurred most likely farther west, in the regions of Indo-European nomadism. Still, the movements of the capital indicate that, at the start of their reign, the Shang people (like the Germanic peoples moving into the failing Roman empire) had not yet settled down to the same wholly agricultural and sedentary life characteristic of the people of the plains.

The imposition of Shang authority on north China did not mean pacification. Although some of the conquered people (Hsia?) allied themselves with the Shang and fitted into the new political system, others continued hostilities, perhaps down to Chou times. There is evidence that "Hsia" peoples began moving westward and southward out of the path of the Shang conquerors. Farther west there were the so-called Ch'iang peoples, names of which appear on the oracle bones. There may be some relationship between these people and the Tibetans, for there are indications that the Tibetans moved southward and westward from an earlier location in western China to Tibet. These Ch'iang people may have been in a stage of primitive nomadism, somewhat like the style of life that many Tibetan nomads still lead. During their entire existence, both before and after the founding of the city of Yin, the Shang were threatened by these western tribes. Thus we see that Chinese civilization, one of the most widespread, stable, and continuous in world history, arose from diverse beginnings, in continuous conflict, and in a relatively small area, a segment of what would later become China.

The city of Shang was founded around 1400 B.C. With the establishment of a permanent capital, some immigration of population must have occurred. The highly developed bronze and pottery industry needed a permanent urban population.

Excavations have shown the remains of walls far from the supposed centers of the settlement. Vestiges of drains, probably used to take water out of the city into the nearby river, indicate a city of considerable size. However, there were few buildings of any imposing size. There were hundreds of pits and cellars, doubtless the homes of the ordinary members of the population, around the peripheries of the city. Roofs were flat, and the tops of the pit houses protruded only a little above the ground. The houses of the nobility were larger and apparently built of mud supported by wooden beams. However, they too were relatively small. Beyond the confines of the city were the fields. Although agriculture was the main occupation of the Shang people, there is little to indicate that irrigation was already in widespread use in the early Shang period. Farming was probably extensive, involving enormous tracts of land. But the pressure to support a growing urban population may have forced technological advances toward the middle and end of the period. By the end of the Shang era, irrigation and river canals may have been in use.

It is not easy to reconstruct the nature of society during Shang times. Both the legends and the oracle bones indicate that there was some form of tribal organization, perhaps totemistic, during this period. The Shang people were the ruling tribe among a large number of tribes, some allied with the Shang, some hostile. Each of these tribes seemed to have occupied specific regions and presumably exercised political control over them. The supreme figure in Shang society was the king or *wang*. The kings were direct, lineal descendants of the founders of the tribe. Succession did not at first proceed by primogeniture (i.e., eldest son to eldest son), but agnatically (i.e., elder brother to younger brother). However, it is hard to say whether agnatic succession was the rule or simply the fact. Among other primitive tribal peoples the tribal ruler is often selected by the tribal oligarchs in some sort of deliberative assembly, and this may have been the case also among the Shang. But as time passed, the custom of succession by primogeniture became more fixed in Shang society. Primogeniture went hand in hand with the growing consolidation of the political system, the growth of the city, and the hardening of social stratification.

Later Chinese historians regarded the Shang kings as links in a chain of legitimate succession going back to the times of the remote mythical emperors. The need to prove the continuity of legitimate rule — the "correct line" (*cheng-t'ung*) as it was later known — was a crucial part of Confucian political philosophy. Yet, there is no indication that the Shang king considered himself the sole legitimate ruler of the universe, as was the case with later emperors. There are references in the oracle bone inscriptions to *wang* other than the Shang Wang. These were apparently rulers of states with which the Shang were in conflict. Unlike the later emperors, the Shang king did not lead a life remote from his subjects in imposing palaces. He seems to have shared the life of the ordinary tribal aristocracy, much like a nomadic chief.

However, in a society dominated by strong religious and magical beliefs, the *wang* was not only a chief, but the supreme shaman, who carried out sacrifices and performed rites of divination. He was thus the holder of magical powers. These were transmitted through him to his successors. Max Weber has written often of this problem in terms of the transmission of "charisma," that mystic power through which rulers elicit obedience from their followers. One can thus see, in these early problems of succession, the seeds of the later imperial and Confucian question of royal and dynastic succession.

One of the chief classes of the city of Yin seems to have been that of the shamans, whose chief function was to maintain the diverse rites characterizing the religious life of Shang. Divinations were carried out before any great undertaking, such as a military expedition. Harvest forecasts were favorite subjects for divination. The Shang people saw the universe as populated by a variety of divine forces that had to be sometimes propitiated, sometimes solicited for aid and information for tasks whose outcomes were problematical. The shaman class in many ways seems to have played the role of a civil bureaucracy, though of a primitive sort. The later Classics, when speaking of scholars like Confucius who attended upon the rulers of their day, imply that scholar-bureaucrats (like I-yin, who served T'ang, the founder of the Shang dynasty) had been available as advisers to the

kings since earliest antiquity. There certainly were no litera-
ti-bureaucrats of later Confucian type during these primeval
periods of Chinese history; here, again, the relation of legend to fact must be considered. But it is not impossible that
some of the magical-religious awe with which the people of
the Shang era viewed their shamans may later have been
transmitted to the scholar-bureaucrat class. In fact, some
contemporary descriptions of nineteenth-century China refer to the local magistrate as a kind of shaman who performed magical rituals for the population under his control.

In many ways, the religious beliefs of the Shang people
are similar to animistic beliefs common to most agricultural
peoples in the early stages of their development. There were
sacrifices to the various spirits of nature — the "wind and
water," as they were later known in China — that could exercise benevolent or malevolent influences on the harvest.
But already in Shang times we have strong evidence for the
ancestor worship that is so characteristic of traditional
China in particular. The Shang state was tribally organized,
and each tribe apparently kept a careful record of its ancestors. There is some evidence that some of these primordial
ancestors were thought of in totem form. The ancestor of
Shang was thought to be a bird, as is indicated in a verse
from the *Book of Songs* (*Shih-ching*, tr. James Legge):
"Heaven commissioned the swallow to descend and give
birth to [the father of our] Shang." Sacrifices were made to
the ancestors, both the remote primordial ancestors and the
more clearly human ancestors. Animals and grain were favorite objects of sacrifice. Liquors, probably prepared from
grains, were often parts of the sacrifices. Thus in China, too,
as elsewhere, the use of intoxicants had a magical-religious
origin.

Even in later times, the descendants of the Shang period
who lived in the more rationalistic period of the Late Chou
remembered the intense religious atmosphere of the earlier
period. Belief in the "gods" (*shen*) and the "spirits" (*kuei*)
was referred to in the Classics, and it remained fundamental
in Chinese folk religion. The *shen* are the divine deities in-
herent in the objects of nature, and the *kuei* are the spirits
of ancestors, who, in disembodied form, remain in the vicin-
ity of the areas where once they lived.

Before we move on from the subject of religion, mention must be made of one religious belief that may have been peculiar to the Shang people. This was the belief in some form of supreme heavenly deity — the *ti* — a word used later to designate the emperors of the country. References to *ti* in contexts of divination reveal that he was regarded as a supreme being reigning over all the divine forces of the cosmos, and the deity to whom question of utmost gravity were addressed. In origin, *ti* may have been the name for one of the Shang ancestors. The Chou, who conquered the Shang, had their own deity, called *t'ien* (Heaven), who in the early Chou documents which we possess, is regarded as equivalent to *ti*. *T'ien,* originally the pictograph of a great man, may have acquired the sense of deity because it was used to refer to the dead Chou kings on high.

This worship of a supreme heavenly deity is also found among many steppe nomads of later times. In fact, the Turco-Mongolian word for heaven, *tengri,* is thought to have some etymological relationship to the Chinese word, *t'ien.* In the West, monotheism, if not a product of the desert, as Renan thought, at least seems to have developed and found favor among peoples who had some nomadic or tribal histories. Here, too, the belief in a supreme heavenly deity may indicate some connection with tribal groups to the north and east, groups from which the later Turks and Mongols may also have sprung. Belief in such a deity, however, clearly had its earthly uses. The charisma of the Shang kings was based in large part on their ability, as augurs, to communicate with the supreme being, *ti*. And it was part of the Chou propaganda to persuade the conquered Shang that *ti* (or *t'ien*) had commanded their downfall. Thus we find Chou accounts of Shang history in which *t'ien* is depicted, anachronistically, as a Shang deity, reproving and punishing unworthy Shang rulers. This was bad history, but useful political dogma. The idea that a special relationship existed between the secular ruler and the all-powerful deity remained central to later Chinese political thought. The ruler meditated between man and heaven, and any rebel who dared to oppose the ruler was opposing the will of heaven itself.

Besides the considerable group of shamans, there was an

even larger class of nobles. Some of these nobles were tribal aristocrats, related by blood or alliance to the Shang ruling house. Some of them apparently were members of different tribes, sometimes at war with the Shang and at other times in submission. Some members of the nobility may also have been aboriginal chiefs allowed to enter the ranks of the conquering elite. Some nobles lived in or near Shang. Many more lived in their "countries," *kuo*. The Chinese term *kuo*, which now means country, apparently had a different meaning in those times. It seems to have designated a city or fortified settlement as well as the territory that surrounded it (today, too, the word *hsien* designates both a district and the capital city of a district). These *kuo* began to develop during the years of conquest and continued to develop during the latter years of Shang. Thus, by Chou times, much of north China must have been covered with settlements of this sort, which became the centers of the later "states" of the Chou period.

It is not entirely clear how the Shang kings exercised political control over the nobility. We know that Shang kings kept powerful armies, and that military expeditions seem to have been constant, as the oracle bones attest. The nobles were undoubtedly called upon to provide armies for such expeditions, and the existence of common foes helped maintain solidarity between distant nobility and the court. Where such solidarity broke down, the Shang kings had enough power to punish the rebels. If warfare was not in progress, the kings were often engaged in large-scale hunting expeditions, another indication of the forest tribal origin of the Shang. It is curious that the Chinese word for cultivated field, *t'ien* (not the same character as the *t'ien* for "Heaven"), seems to have meant a hunting preserve in those days. The usefulness of hunts to reinforce solidarity among the nobility was repeatedly demonstrated in medieval western Europe and Russia, as well as in other areas.

In the city of Yin itself, there must have been many artisans among the considerable population. If we can judge from practices in other societies, the artisans were held in high esteem. But we know little about them except their products. There were large numbers of slaves, most if not all of them prisoners taken in military expeditions (there are many references to Ch'iang or possibly proto-Tibetan prisoners). As we have suggested, Chinese Communist historians see in references to slaves proof of the existence of a slave-based society and economy, in the classic pattern delineated by Engels. However, there is no evidence to indicate that slaves played any important role in agriculture. The Romans employed slaves on a large scale because their *latifundia* were market-oriented, and a fluid and flexible labor force was necessary to meet the changing demands of the market. No such situation existed in north China during Shang times. As in later times, slaves were probably employed in various capacities in and near the court, or were reimpressed into the armies of the king.

We have no evidence whatever of life in the villages. All records pertain solely to life in and around the court. However, there are some things we can infer from available sources. Compact villages definitely existed. Millet and barley, and perhaps rice, were cultivated. The water buffalo was already in use as a domestic animal, although we do not know in what manner. The large numbers of stone sickles found at An-yang and other Shang sites may have been manufactured, stored, and issued to the peasants by the royal house. The existence of a great city and a far-flung tribal nobility suggests that the peasants must have been under considerable pressure to part with any surplus. In the later Classics, there is talk of the "well-field" system that supposedly prevailed in antiquity. According to this system, fields were divided into nine squares; the produce of eight of them went to the peasants, and that of the ninth to the lord.

It is highly likely that exploitation in the form of a fraction of the yield did in fact exist. The level of productivity was not high at that time; hence, only a small surplus would have been left to extract. We know from other societies that in areas where agricultural productivity is low, as in high mountain regions, peasants tend to own their own land. It is only in areas of relatively high productivity that one finds landlordism. Although it is unlikely that concepts of ownership were highly defined in those times, the peasants were probably "free" rather than "servile," land-owning (in a modest way) rather than bound to the land. The life of the ordinary peasant must have been close to the subsistence level, and the villages of an extremely primitive sort. It was only during the latter part of the Chou (near the end of the first millenium B.C.) that villages could have taken on a substantial appearance. For it was then that new technological developments, such as the introduction of iron and wheat, began to change the life on the land.

Reading

Creel, Herrlee Glessner, *The Birth of China: A Study of the Formative Period of Chinese Civilization* (Ungar: Chicago, 1964). Paperback (original edition 1937). Where it converges in subject matter with Chang Kwang-chih, *The Archaeology of Ancient China* (see Chapter 6) the latter is to be preferred, since Chang had access to later research.

Implications

Historical Particularity and Historical Analogy

It would appear from the description of Shang society that the Shang began by moving their capital from place to place, like Central Asian nomads and early Japanese emperors; that the Shang resembled the ancient Germans in their conquests and infiltration; that Shang religion had some of the animistic quality of religious systems obtaining among many early agricultural peoples, and some of the proto-monotheistic quality of many early nomadic peoples' religions; that for the Shang kings and nobles, as for their counterparts in medieval Europe, the hunt was a means of solidarity. Do such cross-cultural comments prejudice the particularity of Chinese history in this, its early stage? Or, if Shang culture can be vindicated as highly individual, are such comments merely mischievous rhetorical flourishes?

If we grasp the essential point that any society is a complex, a whole that is something other than the sum of its parts, we know that items of analogy do not compromise the particularity of Shang or any other historical culture. Cultural differentiation, which attends the emergence from prehistory and creates for historical man his historical sense, his consciousness of *inheritance* or cultural continuity, is a matter of wholes, not parts: horizontal lines out from Shang to foreign cultures cannot confuse the "Chineseness" of the central core. We have indicated that Shang is a *Chinese* beginning, a point on a vertical line of continuity through time. More is gathered together in Shang than is held in common by Shang and anyone non-Chinese. Shang, for example, may have come into the "Hsia" world like the Germans into Rome — but (in spite of what the later legends represent as fact) Hsia, unlike Rome, was not a sophisticated, complicated empire in decay. The Shang-Hsia amalgam, therefore, was very different from the German-Roman. Only in a Confucian conceptual scheme was Hsia an "empire"; but Rome was an empire in historical fact.

Yet, though the wholes differ, any similarities between Chinese and foreign parts, in the Shang or any age, are worthy of comment. The individual is not just preserved by the fact that the similarities are only *partial*; it is this partial character that helps one to identify the individual's particular quality. For what is really the point of coupling Shang and tribal Germans in one discussion, as the similarity of their careers of infiltration may prompt us to do? The point is to pique us to realize how comparison is possible but full analogy fails: the triumph of Shang was nothing like the "triumph of barbarism and religion" that Gibbon, though overdramatically, thought he discerned in Rome. Shang, after all, established — it did not destroy — that Chinese civilization whose characteristic mission was the destruction of barbarism.

Time had to pass before Shang could be identified as the point of departure for civilization in China. But passing time — and particularity — are the historian's concerns. A similarity of static types dissolves in time, as they become dynamic and individual: Shang conquest plus state-building, as a process in time, is *not* similar to German conquest plus state-dissolving. The dynamic process involved in the "plus" is what individuates. And the static *universal* involved in identical definition ("conquest") is what poses the question of why the *particular* dynamically emerges.

In the great subject of feudalism in China, we shall find the historical problem of analogy and process most insistently brought to the fore.

4

Background

The "Western Chou"

CHOU ORIGINS AND CONQUEST

The city of Yin prospered, agriculture and technology developed, and Chinese culture took on a more substantial form. But turbulence arose in the lands to the north and west of China. It was during the second millenium B.C. that Indo-European tribes with pastoral nomadic habits began to sweep down from what is now the Ukraine into Iran and India. Other branches of Indo-Europeans seem to have swept eastwards into what is now western China and perhaps as far east as Mongolia. Scythian tombs with objects remarkably similar wherever they occur — the animal art, for instance — have been found in a wide arc from Manchuria to eastern Europe. As late as the first millenium A.D. the regions of Khotan and Kashgar were inhabited by Iranian peoples. Persian-speaking Tadjiks are to this day still found in the eastern Pamirs, within the borders of China. The turbulence aroused by the nomads spread still farther east, where it began pulling proto-Turks and proto-Mongols out of the forests and turning them into nomads. The rise of steppe nomadism, with all the consequences it would have for the huge sedentary societies of Eurasia, was one of the great processes of world history.

If it is unlikely that the Shang people were nomads or influenced by nomadism, there are indications that the Chou people may have had some more direct contacts with nomads and nomadism. Unlike the Shang people, the Chou people originated in the northwestern parts of China. When they first appear in history, they were settled along the reaches (and perhaps to the west) of the Wei River valley, then the western frontier of Chinese (Shang) influence. Earlier they seem to have been settled in the southwestern parts of modern Kansu province, closer to the steppes. Though we have no indication that the Chou were fundamentally alien to the people of the Shang regions, there are, as we have seen, some indications of ethnic and cultural differences.

Chinese legends regard the Chou as the descendants of [Chi] Hou-chi, one of the ministers of Shun and Yü. His son is said to have lost his position at the court and fled to the land of the I and Ti (the northern and western barbarians), where his family records were lost. During Shang times, the Chou line reappears in the form of one Kung Liu, who, though still living among the barbarians, relearns the agricultural arts once taught to the Chou people by their ancestor, Hou-chi (whose name means "millet king"), but since forgotten. Kung Liu's son then completes the transition to settled agricultural life by establishing himself and his people in the country of Pin, on the Wei River in modern Shensi province (or in modern Shansi? — the location is very uncertain). The legends seem to indicate some foreign, perhaps quasi-nomadic origin. Some historians see in the name of Hou-chi's mother, Chiang-yüan, signs of a relationship with the barbarian Ch'iang peoples of Shang times. Whatever the case may be, there seems little doubt that the Chou people were not simply sedentary people of the "Hsia" type. Like their Shang predecessors, they were most likely originally tribally organized and to some extent mobile. This mobility aided them in their later conquest of eastern China.

The Shang conquests in the east brought about a gradual movement of population westward. These westward-moving people probably mixed with the eastward moving Chou, and thus brought them into contact with the dominant cultures of north China. The Chou people spent a considerable time in Shensi before their conquest of Shang, a time in which they were apparently sedentary and agricultural. By the conquest period, the Chou had acquired the political capacity to lead a federation of tribal nations against the dominant Shang, and they must have developed their own relatively sophisticated bronze-working industry. Some scholars think that the Chou brought in iron from Central Asia to China; others, probably more correctly, do not think so. Incontrovertibly, however, the introduction of iron ploughs (and winter wheat) during the late Chou period brought about an economic revolution in Chinese farming.

We do not know what induced the Chou to undertake conquest of the Shang territories. Threatened by nomad attacks from the north and west, the Chou sharpened their military power. Centuries later a successor to Chou, the Ch'in state, which was also situated in the wilds of Shensi, developed its military might as a result of constant nomadic attack. The threatened border lands of China tended to produce powerful, rugged peoples, who sometimes turned their power inward against the softer, more protected Chinese heartland.

If Kung Liu brought about the reorganization and strengthening of the Chou people, it was Wen Wang, the "Lettered" or the "Civilized King" who is supposed to have begun the conquest of Shang. Wen Wang (probably largely a *post-facto* idealization) has been celebrated in traditional Chinese lore as the epitome of the wise ruler, who challenged, in his innate goodness, the evil last ruler of the Shang, Shou Hsin.* Shou Hsin was accused (in the *Book of Documents* [*Shu-ching*], tr. James Legge) of being "abandoned to drunkenness and reckless in lust. . . . He has burned and roasted the loyal and good. He has ripped up pregnant women." It was the later Chinese ideological bias that demanded that failure be ascribed to evil. Nevertheless, it is likely that Shou Hsin, the scion of an old ruling house, was at least inept and faltering compared to the dynamic men from the west. By the time of the death of Wen Wang,

---

* His royal title was Chou, the same romanization but a different character from that of the Chou dynasty. In order to avoid confusing this Shang monarch with the Chou who ousted him, we will continue to refer to him as Shou Hsin, his personal name.

most of the Shang lands had been brought under Chou control.

The conquest of the Shang territories was completed by Wen Wang's son, Wu Wang, the "Military King" and first monarch of the formally proclaimed Chou dynasty. During the reign of his successor, the young king Ch'eng Wang, a revolt of remnants of the Shang ruling house and some of its adherents took place. The revolt was soon put down and all resistance ended. Long before the end of the fighting with the Shang, Wu Wang and his younger brother (and regent for his successor), the "Duke of Chou," undertook the organization of a new type of political and social system. It was to remain the dominant system for several hundred years. This system has often been described as feudalism.

SOCIAL ORGANIZATION

When the Chou conquered the Shang (ca. 1000 B.C.) they found a developed civilization along the lower reaches of the Yellow River. A great city, Yin — the capital of an "empire" — was the focal point of that civilization. Writing and the keeping of records were known. A large class of priests and officials lived in the city. Agriculture was highly developed. Trade brought large quantities of luxury goods into the city. However, the political power of the great city had not been applied to an equally complex organizing of the hinterland. The Shang exerted their power largely through the periodic launching of punitive expeditions into hostile areas. When these areas had been pacified, the armies left garrisons behind or withdrew to the city. From time to time the king would sally forth with his retinue to "hunt," presumably in special preserves (*t'ien*, etymologically related, as we have suggested, to the later word for field); in such fashion the ruler made his authority felt among the surrounding peoples.

It was the absence of organized Shang control that permitted the Chou to rise slowly in the remote western lands of Shensi, in the fertile lands of the Han and Wei River valleys. When their power was great enough, they moved east and subjugated the Shang. The Chou presumably had the choice of occupying the old capital and ruling from there or selecting a new site for their political center. They chose the latter course. It is not clear why. Perhaps the great city had been so thoroughly destroyed in war that reconstruction was difficult. Perhaps the Chou distrusted the subdued population and felt insecure in the capital of their enemies. Perhaps defeat had put a magical-religious stigma on the site. Most likely the Chou felt the pressure of nomads on the frontier, and responded by marshaling their strength in a frontier capital, not in the economic heartland of Honan. They established their capital in their own homeland, Shensi, and proceeded to organize their newly conquered domains from there.

The Chou devised a system of permanent control and eschewed the more casual practices of the Shang. Several factors forced the development of a stable political system. The dangerous frontier of the west, which time and again felt the pressure of nomadic groups (only dimly visible in the fragments of historical material), demanded the maintenance of a large western army for defense. The prosperity of the Shang had led to the development of new, incipient centers of power, particularly to the south, where later the state of Ch'u (in its beginnings non-Chinese in culture) would arise. Military means alone could not permanently ensure stability. The answer to the problem of control was found in the *feng-chien* system of enfeoffment.

During the period of the two great dynastic founders, Wu Wang and the subsequent regent, the "Duke of Chou" (in traditional Chinese historiography, a paragon of virtue), north China was marked out into some hundred areas. The personal domain of the Chou ruler extended from modern Shensi down the Yellow River into Honan (the second capital at Lo-yang was built by the Duke of Chou). The areas of the semicircle to the east and south were allocated to members of the Chou royal family and to their intimate allies. Farther to the east, in Honan, the Chou enfeoffed members of the Shang royal family in an area known as Sung. But surrounding the potentially hostile Sung, they established appanages that were granted to members of the Chou family, such as the appanage of Lu* (later the home

* In the beginning, only a short stretch of Lu's boundary was contiguous with Sung.

state of Confucius), which was given to the descendants of the Duke of Chou. In this way the available political elite of the Shang was used to rule areas of eastern China, but close by were the lands of the conquerors, to counterbalance the Shang and prevent insurrection. One finds the same policy of check and balance described in the ancient Indian political theory of "circle rule" (*mandala*). Much later, in Tokugawa Japan (seventeenth–nineteenth centuries), the "shogunate" strategically placed its allies (the *fudai*) and its erstwhile enemies (the *tōzama*, "the outsiders") in such a way as to counterbalance one another.

The lords of these hundred or so domains became the nobility of Chou China; they were the top stratum of a stratified society. Peasants, at the bottom, went with the land. Whoever had the land had them, though the peasants had certain claims on its produce.

Each domain was constituted on the model of the imperial domain. The lords had full political and economic control of the region. Small administrative and garrison towns grew up as the domain's political centers. Each lord appointed officials — *tai-fu* — to administer subsidiary areas, and below the *tai-fu* there were other functionaries. Ties between the lord and his officials were not yet impersonal, bureaucratic. Many of these lower officials, particularly in the early period, were collateral kinsmen, related by blood to the lord's lineage. In fact, the domain system of administration was closely tied in with the prevalent kinship system.

Already in their formative period, the Chou had developed socioreligious orientations toward lineage; therefore, the kinship system that ultimately evolved in China (and that involved ancestor worship) was later given the name of this lineage system, *tsung-fa*, a term with religious implications. A sacred line of descent was believed to pass down from generation to generation, always through the eldest son. The families that clustered around the bearer of the lineage were known as the main families, the *ta-tsung*. But farther out, the collateral relatives — the younger brothers and their descendants — were part of the lineage as minor families, *hsiao-tsung*. Sib ties remained strong, for the collateral relatives were bound to their "main families" through the solidarity of common descent and worship of common ancestors. It was from this group of collateral families of the lords that the local officials of the domains were recruited.

Though the kinship ties between the Chou royal family and the feudatories became more attenuated as time went on (for as the lines of descent widened, erstwhile minor families constituted themselves into new main families), other institutionalized practices served to maintain bonds between the Chou king and his lordly subjects. Each lord had to swear oaths of fealty to the monarch, had to make periodic obeisance to the king, had to furnish military aid when the king required it, and had to be re-enfeoffed as he assumed the rank and position of his father. Though the Chou ruler remained in his capital, the lords came to him from time to time, thus maintaining close personal ties.

If the feudal system of the early Chou was the first attempt at organized political control of a large area, one must admit that it succeeded. But success was impermanent, and by the eighth century B.C. the process of breakdown began. With the murder of the monarch in 771 B.C., the capital was moved east to Lo-yang, and the "Eastern Chou" period of imperial impotence began. Increasingly, until the traumatic reunification in 221 B.C., China was gripped in a never-ending series of wars, during which the old order began to disappear. As the power of the Chou court waned, the states — the *kuo* — became increasingly independent. On the periphery of the empire, from the northeast westward and then to the south, new states arose and absorbed the older feudal appanages. The royal throne became the object of competitive conflict, as the states sought the prestige of the king to advance their own ends and check their enemies. Political conflict ran parallel with social and economic development. Vertical social mobility increased in pace. Population moved into new regions. Agriculture advanced with the introduction of wheat and a two-crop economy. The introduction of iron revolutionized both agriculture and warfare. As in Europe, the decline of feudalism was a stage of bloody conflict and remarkable material progress. We shall soon turn from the essentially static description of "system" to this dynamic problem of "stage."

Reading

Bodde, Derk, "Feudalism in China" in Coulborn, Rushton (ed.),
Feudalism in History (Archon Books: Hamden, Connecticut
1965). Paperback (original edition 1956).

Implications

The Problem of Historical Analogy:
(a) Feudalism as System

It has become commonplace among students of Chinese
history to label the age of the Chou as a feudal age. China
during the first half of the first millenium B.C. seemed to
show similarities in its social and political systems to the
regime existing in Europe during the early centuries of the
second millenium A.D. In both these regions, far removed
from each other in time and space, there seemed to be con-
figurations of social relations relating to an ideal type that
scholars called feudalism. Perhaps the institution that above
all suggested the similarity was the fief (in Latin, *feodum*,
from which the term "feudalism" derives). Chou China, like
Europe, had its fiefs, known as "apportioned lands" *(fen-ti)*.
The Chinese language also had the term, *feng-chien,** meaning to allocate a delineated region to an individual and to
establish him as the legitimate ruler there. Scholars chose
this term, *feng-chien* (and *chih-tu*, system) to translate the
European "feudalism." Medieval Europe and pre-Ch'in
China both seemed to possess regimes that were somehow
related to a universal ideal type.

But does the old adage, *traditore traduttore* ("to trans-

* *feng*: originally meant, apparently, a raised earthen mound at
which ceremonies were conducted and which was used to mark boundaries. *chien*: to set up.

late is to betray"), perhaps apply? In what sense (and in what sense only) are we justified in suggesting this historical analogy?

In itself, the designation of the pre-Ch'in period as the feudal age committed the western scholar, and the Chinese scholars who accepted this view, to a vision of Chinese history far different from that of the orthodox Confucianist. Chou China was the historical source of the model society that Confucius advocated in the carefully edited texts he submitted for posterity. Later Confucianists looked upon this society as one that not only had really existed, but as the model for all good societies. All existing societies represented in one form or another a deviation from this norm. No utopian imagery was needed to paint the outlines of the good society. It was there, fully described, in the classic texts.

But the modern designation of the pre-Ch'in age as feudal (i.e., as *one* type of empirically observable society, not as *the* type of all good societies) drove a wedge between two segments of Chinese history, a wedge more serious than the simple dynastic periodization that was already current among the Chinese. It asserted that there was a qualitative difference in different periods of Chinese history. The early Ch'ing thinker, Wang Fu-chih (1619–1692), had dared to suggest such an idea, and he had been proscribed as unorthodox. Only late-nineteenth- and twentieth-century Chinese writers, who themselves had assented to the transformation of absolute values into relative products of history, rehabilitated this erstwhile heretic. Certainly, earlier thinkers (most notably the great Sung neo-Confucian philosopher, Chu Hsi, 1130–1200) had distinguished the Chou period from later periods and denied the possibility of reestablishing Chou institutions. But, to such thinkers, it was not a question of historical evolution but one of moral decline: whatever the actual possibilites, Chou was an ideal type.

For the Occidental, feudalism denotes the formative period for modern Europe. Out of feudalism came the nation-state, and out of the nation-state the forces of modern capitalism. Implicitly, the European studying China, and the Chinese scholar using western, post-Confucian categories, stamped the mark of "stage" on the Chou period in calling it feudal. But a stage towards what? Apparently, it was a step on the road to the constitution of "traditional China," that China still well known to westerners of the nineteenth century, and the China that has crumbled completely only in recent times. But this was not the road that included the feudal stage in Europe.

One may look at a fragment of history in two different ways. One may see it in its own light, as a period whose very existence proclaims the viability of its political, social, and cultural structures; one tries, then, to discover the patterns that made it a workable system. Or one may see it as a transitional period, one in which old structures are disappearing, the patterns dissolving, to make room for new. Stability and change are the two great phenomena that the past always shows. The Chou dynasty lasted almost a full millennium, from its inception through conquest during the eleventh century B.C. until its demise through conquest in the third century B.C. It was more or less bisected by an event that saw the center of imperial power shift from the western frontier to an eastern point safely embedded in the heart of the society. During its first period it achieved stability, and we can see the outlines of a universal system, the basis of analogy. During its latter period it was visibly in its slow stage of decline and change, and historical particulars must recall us to the individual.

Our concern here is with the initial stage, when the system "worked." It is for this period, contemporary with Assyria and Minoan Crete and long antedating the rise of Hellenistic, Roman, and Indian empires, that a connection has been posited with an ideal type called feudalism. Scholars have seen evidences of feudalism not only in western Europe and Chou China, but in Japan, the Arab and Turkish empires, and post-Kievan Russia. The Russian scholar, Vladimirtsov, even created (for purposes of Marxist exposition), the term, "nomadic feudalism," for the regime of the Turkish and Mongol nomads of the Central Asian steppes. Feudalism, then, is an analytic term; through its careful application the particulars of histories may be related to universals.

Marxists, we noted, have made the sweeping assumption that these universals are operative in all historical contexts, and they have established a scheme of historical evolution in which feudalism has its inevitable place. But for some latter-day Marxists feudalism does not characterize Chou China; the earlier stage, "slave society," is said to have persisted from Shang through Chou. For the contemporary Chinese communist historians, the feudatory of Chinese history is not so much the Chou noble as the gentry landowner of later periods. The Marxist view is unacceptable to most western scholars, because it squeezes the particulars of history into a rigid developmental scheme. The rigidity of the scheme reflects the classic error of the doctrinaire: the bending of particulars to conform with one's own universals.

One must be wary, then, of universalizing in either the Marxist or Platonic fashion, either warping the facts to fit the model or using a model to transcend the facts. On the other hand, rank empiricism — the meticulous arranging of facts without any principle of understanding — does not bring us understanding. The study of history must be a dialectic between universal and particular, between the ideas and images that scholars create so as to order discrete facts, and the particulars that a scholar knows through immersion in specific historical situations. Thus, for our purposes, we can propose certain ideas and constructs as "universals" in the historical situations that we are comparing, but at the same time we must mark out the differences between the situations, and between concepts and descriptions.

If one glances quickly at European feudalism and the reputed feudalisms of other societies, one salient observation can be made: the systems represent patterns of allocation and maintenance of political power. Feudal systems are thus essentially political systems. But they are political systems of a particular sort. Since Montesquieu, the view has become widespread that the essence of the systems of early medieval Europe was the fief. A fief — or *beneficium*, as it was known in an earlier Latin form — was a delineated territory allocated to an individual who might exercise limited or unlimited control over it. In Merovingian and Carolingian Europe, the system of fiefs arose at a time of political disunity, tribal movements, intermittent warfare, breakdown of supraregional political, economic, social, and cultural ties. Feudalism arose during a period of fragmentation, induced

37

by the breakdown of the Roman order and the settling of northern Europe. But during this period there arose several supraregional conquest kingdoms. Without the existence of a bureaucracy or a settled social order, the new monarchies relied on the institution of the fief for the maintenance of control. Fiefs were given to followers of the conqueror. From the fiefs these warriors drew their sustenance, not only to live but to have the means for waging war. They were bound by ties of *hominium et fidelitas*, the duty to provide military aid to the ruler and the obligation of everlasting loyalty. These ties have been called the ties of vassalage. The eminent French historian, Marc Bloch, has called these two institutions, *fief* and *vassalage*, the two major elements of medieval European feudalism.

The political system that arose on the foundation of the fief was one through which large territories were marked off and parceled out to members of conquering elites. Politically, the map of Europe was a patchwork quilt with central patches, more or less extensive, indicating seats of monarchies. Beyond the borders of Europe we do indeed find political systems that have these characteristics. Where they exist, they are associated usually with conquest in weakly organized, weakly bureaucratized societies. The Mongols of the steppe were strongly tied to one another, hierarchically, by ties of personal obligation, and when they conquered the lands of central and western Asia in the twelfth and thirteenth centuries A.D., their rulers parceled out the lands in a feudal manner. (So they did in China, although, as we shall see, the attempt failed dramatically. They conquered China in the thirteenth century, but China in that day was not a weakly organized and weakly bureaucratized state.) In Japan, beginning in the tenth century A.D., piecemeal conquest of the southwest — the land of tradition and the court — by the wild northeast, the motherland of the warrior *samurai*, brought about fiefal situations, as the samurai obtained control of the earlier manors (much as the Frankish warrior nobility intruded on the lands of Gallo-Roman landowners). The ties of personal super- and subordination that held the feudal structure together are still reflected in the rich Japanese vocabulary relating to obligation to authority: *on, giri, gimu*. The Turks of Seljuq times in Iran (eleventh and twelfth centuries) distributed "cut-off lands" (*iqtas*) to their cohorts. In sixteenth-century Russia, Ivan IV ("the Terrible") destroyed the boyars and set up a new regime based on land grants (*pomest'e*) to his soldiers; only later, with the Romanovs, did a bureaucracy develop. Thus, the essentials of a feudal type, the essentials of a timeless, formal system, can be found repeated in different times and places — however differently they finally responded to the ravages of time.

The maintenance of these personal bonds, these ties of super- and subordination, were crucial to the preservation of the feudal system. But the feudal system in Europe declined. As the system of inheritance through primogeniture arose, it served a dual, contradictory function. On the one hand, it preserved the integrity of the fiefal lands, but on the other hand it weakened the power of personal tie to ruler and lord. This system of inheritance nurtured a hereditary aristocracy. Personal ties began to be supplanted by contractual ties — for example, on a large scale, *Magna Carta*. Law supplanted custom. But as the aristocracy rose as a class, monarchy also developed as a powerful institution. From its nadir in post-Carolingian times, monarchy became stronger in countries such as France and England. In Germany, though national unity was absent, local states began to arise that gathered more and more erstwhile feudal domains under their control. The hostile confrontation of monarchy and aristocracy marks the history of Europe until the triumph of monarchical absolutism, early in France and Austria, later in Prussia. In England, a balance was institutionalized. The feudal system had had its stage in European history.

Stage aside, Chou China had surely approximated the system. The situation in China during the eleventh century B.C. has its similarities to the situation of the Frankish tribes not long after the fall of Rome. Both the Chou peoples and the Franks conquered areas of preexisting civilizations. In both instances, the conquerors were unable to rule through their own bureaucracies, nor did the situation allow it. Both were warrior peoples. The Franks were victors in innumerable tribal wars, the Chou had grown strong fighting on the periphery of the Chinese world. What calls our attention to these similarities is the similarity between the political systems that ensued in both histories.

In both, the royal courts that initially created the system declined to insignificance, while aristocracy increased its power. Marc Bloch speaks of the factor of heredity, in particular primogeniture, as ultimately subversive of the feudal system. In China, too, the lineage system, *tsung-fa*, ultimately gave rise to local, hereditary aristocracies, as the blood ties to the Chou became more remote. The Chou lords, in fact, assumed independent surnames, from which most modern Chinese surnames derive. Hereditary titles and ranks among the *tai-fu* of the various states did not exist in the early "model" period of Chou, but were a late innovation in the "Spring and Autumn" period (q.v.); they are symbolic of the decline of the *feng-chien* system.

Two elements that have been singled out as essential in the feudalism of Europe were also present in early Chou China: fiefdom and vassalage. In both instances, a political system based on these two institutions enabled a conquering group to maintain control over a large, dispersed area. In both cases, feudal rule was the precursor of more complex forms of stable political control. And in both cases feudalism, though it brought relative stability for a time, ultimately gave rise to massive conflicts. Out of one, modern Europe emerged — out of the other, bureaucratic-monarchical China, an antitype to modern Europe.

Emergence implies stage. If analogous systems are stages on different roads, does this imply impairment of the analogy? We shall soon see, in any case, how the historian serves a proper purpose in proposing the analogy.

Background

Incipient Feudal Breakdown: the "Spring and Autumn" and Confucius

The feudal ideal is unity, with a pyramid of obligations tapering off to a single sovereign figure at the top. By the eight century B.C., the honoring of any such obligations in Chou China had waned. Princes, especially after the movement of the capital east to Loyang, in 771 B.C., became absolute masters in their feudal states, the *kuo*; no local royal official existed who could intervene. The prince, not the Chou *wang* or king, made good his powers of official appointment. What inhibited the prince's power was not an imperial check from above but a trend below toward transmission by inheritance, so that men of rank and office below the princely developed their own prerogatives, and new fiefs hived off from the old ones. With the "Spring and Autumn" (*Ch'un-ch'iu*) period (722–481 B.C.), soon followed by the age of the "Warring States" (403–221 B.C.), almost all pretense of unity vanished, and autonomous fragments, sometimes pasted together in various expedient alliances, were hurled against each other.

The "Spring and Autumn" period takes its name from a chronicle, "Spring and Autumn Annals of the State of Lu." Confucius (551–479 B.C.), a native of Lu (in modern Shantung province), arranged this cryptic account of the reigns of twelve successive Lu rulers, all of them implicated in the internecine warfare of the times. Why did Confucius do it? Mencius (372–289 B.C.) wrote (tr. James Legge): "The world fell into decay, and principles faded away. Perverse speakings and oppressive deeds waxed rife again. There were instances of ministers who murdered their sovereigns, and of sons who murdered their fathers. Confucius was afraid, and made the 'Spring and Autumn.'" Confucius said: "Yes! It is the 'Spring and Autumn' which will make men know me, and it is the 'Spring and Autumn' which will make men condemn me." According to the tradition, then, Confucius wrote a history of an age of immorality, and wrote it for a moral-didactic purpose. Such was the setting, and such the chosen purpose, of his life.

His family name was K'ung; "Confucius" is a seventeenth-century Jesuit Latinization of the Chinese term of respect, K'ung Fu-tzu, K'ung the Sage, the Master. He was supposed to be descended from a noble family of the Sung state, that preserve that had been left to the superseded Shang by the Chou conquerors. Both parents died when he was young, and he grew up in meager circumstances. He served in minor official posts in Lu, but at the age of 56, despairing of seeing his political philosophy adopted at home, he set out on a decade of wandering to the courts of other states. There, too, he found no real service for him and no political satisfaction. He returned at last to Lu, to resume his only successful pursuits — the inspiration of disciples and the organization of a literature destined to form a canon.

The ideal educational product for Confucius was the *chün-tzu* — the princely man, superior man, or gentleman. The most important ingredients in the *chün-tzu*'s culture were *li* ("ritual", or "decorum" — without the Victorian connotation of primness) and *jen* ("humankindness" — i.e., both "human-kindness" and "humankind-ness"). *Li* represents the aspect of tradition, *jen* the aspect of creative spontaneity. *Li*, that is, relates to outer forms, perpetuated by society and defining the individual's place in the social order. And *jen*, semantically linked to its homonym, the word for "man," relates to the inner quality of humanity (comprehending the "humane" as well as the "human"), the moral nature.

Confucius' disciples divided on the question of emphasis. The objective, "outer" school (including Tzu Yu, Tzu Hsia, and, later, Hsün-tzu) took *li* as central, while the subjective, "inner" school (including Tseng-tzu and, later, Tzu Ssu and Mencius) took *jen* as central (though one could conceivably reverse the attributions, taking *li* as internalizing the sense of propriety and *jen* as externalizing an attitude toward others). Among other concepts embedded in the Confucian ethic are those of *i* (righteousness), *chih* (humane wisdom), *hsin* (trustworthiness), *chung* (loyalty), *hsiao* (filial piety), and *ch'eng* (sincerity). It should be understood that these simple, even banal, English equivalents are much too bare to convey the richness of meaning in the originals. Their contexts in a whole literature must be examined if one is to savor the significance of such terms. The world of concepts in which they participated was a world envisaging a regular cosmic order with which man's conduct should correlate. The classical ethic was essentially natural, depending on neither a divine provenance nor a divine sanction.

The literature that yields these terms and enshrines these ideas is primarily the Classics, treated as a canon first by Confucius, later (with additions and refinements) by Han and Sung Confucianists. The Classics that were traditionally associated with Confucius ultimately came to be called the "Five Classics," as follows:

(1) *Book of Changes (I-ching)*. This is a book of dark wisdom, susceptible of many interpretations. The legendary Fu Hsi, first of the "Three August Ones," was supposed to have made the sixty-four hexagrams (i.e., sixty-four six-line diagrams, made up of various combinations of continuous and broken horizontal lines: these were also used in other ways than those indicated in the *I-ching*). From ancient times it had been used as an oracle book, by the Chou only (the alternate title is *Chou I*, the *Changes of the Chou*) — the Shang had a distinct divination system and tradition, and some others (e.g., Ch'u) had other kinds of analogous practices. As an authoritative text it came to serve the Confucian purpose of discouraging social patronage of ecstatics — human mediums or priestly diviners. Titles like "The

Creative," "The Receptive," "The Darkening Light," are attached to the hexagrams, and several types of texts (including the "Ten Wings," attributed by tradition to Confucius) suggest gnomically the general meaning of the whole work and special meanings of parts. The book contains historical allusions to the Shang period and elements of farmers' folklore. The concept of change projected is that of natural movement, unchanging in itself, precluded from going against nature.

(2) *Book of Documents (Shu-ching)*. This book as we now have it contains several strata, some of them (about half the contents) dating from well after Confucius' day. From Han times on, the question of the relative authenticity of different versions of the *Book of History* was important in Confucian scholarly circles — especially during the Ch'ing dynasty (1644–1912). According to classical tradition, Confucius studied the three thousand official historical documents in the Chou imperial archives and selected one hundred of them to form, with prefaces to each, the *Book of Documents* (the Classic suffered attrition, however, and extant versions are much shorter). This is the *locus classicus*, as we have noted, for the sage-kings Yao, Shun, and Yü, and for the standard Confucian account of the succession from Hsia, through Shang, to Chou — the basic pattern for *ko-ming*, exchange of the "mandate of Heaven." The *Book of Documents* was taken to offer both models of political order and models of literary composition. The direct historical value of at least its earliest stratum is suggested by the fact that, in the corpus of oracle bones recovered, 23 of the 31 Shang rulers listed in *Shu-ching* are mentioned.

(3) *Book of Songs (Shih-ching)*. "Have you studied the *Songs*?" asked Confucius. "If you have not studied the *Songs*, you will not be able to converse." Thus Confucius emphasized the place of this Classic in the gentleman's culture. Confucius is said to have selected 311 poems from about ten times that number to form this anthology of three main types of pieces: folk songs, more sophisticated songs ("lesser" and "greater") composed for formal performance with music, and panegyrics connected with official sacrifices.

(4) *Book of Rites (Li-chi)*. The ancient "rites" literature included four works. The *Li-chi*, one of these, supposed to

be composed of documents transmitted by Confucius, was arranged as a collection by several hands, over a period from the first century B.C. to the second century A.D.; it was not until the twelfth century, during the Sung dynasty, that the *Li-chi* became, retroactively, as it were, *the* "rites" for the canon. Historically the most important of the other three *Rites* texts was the *Institutes of Chou* (*Chou-li* or *Chou-kuan*), attributed (fancifully) to the Duke of Chou. Always a favorite text of strong centralizers, the *Chou-li* outlined in detail what purported to be the Chou empire's centralized system of disposition of officials. The canonical *Book of Rites*, the *Li-chi*, treats of the rites of passage and rules of discipline for social intercourse and cultivated recreation.

(5) *Spring and Autumn Annals* (*Ch'un-ch'iu*), as mentioned earlier. Three "Commentaries" (*chuan*) came to be attached to this text, in ascending order of importance the *Ku-liang chuan, Kung-yang chuan,* and *Tso-chuan* — the latter attributed to one Tso Ch'iu-ming, archivist of Lu and disciple of Confucius. It was the *Tso-chuan* that ultimately became (after a Han dynasty controversy with *Kung-yang* partisans, a controversy revived in the last, the Ch'ing, dynastic period) the one intimately known companion of the *Ch'un-ch'iu.* The *Tso-chuan* is a vivid narrative, more generous with historical information and literary appeal than the bare catalogue, the *Ch'un-ch'iu,* to which it was appended.

Reading

Creel, Herrlee Glessner, *Confucius and the Chinese Way* (New York: Harper Torchbooks, 1960). Paperback (original edition, *Confucius, the Man and the Myth*, 1949).

Implications

Dialectical Change — the Traditionalist as Innovator

The problem of leaders and followers is a famous one in intellectual history. Marx once remarked wryly that he was not a Marxist. Dostoyevsky and Kierkegaard, in mordant moments, saw Christians severed from Jesus. What was the relation between the historical Confucius, an ineffective political adviser in a disintegrating feudal society, and the enormously influential Confucianists in the later highly organized bureaucratic imperial regimes?

These regimes were characteristically autocratic, whereas Confucius (together with followers like Mencius, of a later but still pre-"Confucianist" generation) taught the duty of sovereigns to satisfy the needs of their people. Should we identify Confucius, then, as essentially a popular champion, whose democratic message was distorted by Confucianists?

Many moderns have found this view agreeable, since it colors the central Chinese sage with a celebrated modern value. But this very agreeableness suggests a possible anachronism, the selection of ancient data by modern criteria. After all, why should subsequent thinkers, the Confucianists, have felt it so important to claim Confucius as their sage, if the ideas that they really preferred were not Confucius' at all? His ideas, if unacceptable, presumably fitted him for obscurity. As long as we see the problem of Confucius in the light of a modern concern with a democratic-autocratic dichotomy, we face ourselves with this conundrum, this discontinuity between leader and follower. But in any analysis, if the pieces will fall into a simple picture we ought to prefer it to a complicated one; and Confucius and the Confucianists seem better aligned when we see that *traditionalism*, not democracy, was Confucius' master theme. As we shall see in later chapters, a traditionalist spirit was peculiarly appropriate in a multitude of ways to the post-Confucius imperium, which was the haven of Confucianists.

Yet, we have just begun to probe. Surely it is unsatisfying simply to label Confucius' teaching as traditionalism. For one thing, traditionalism is such a familiar conception, common to so many times and places, that we seem left with the puzzle of greatness. Can Confucius be no more than that, a respectable thinker but almost banal? And for another thing, as a traditonalist, why should it have been he who left that tremendous mark on the historical record — why should it not have been someone behind him, in the past that he himself revered and commended over his own day to the future generations?

There is an answer (extended below) to these two reservations:

a) Although in some minds traditionalism may indeed be only a sentimental preference for other times and other manners, Confucius made it a rich philosophical world view, an all-pervasive commitment to stability over change; it is an ideal sufficiently complex to include his "democratic" recommendations as really just one implication of traditionalism.

b) In elaborating this traditionalism, although it genuinely reflected a reverence for the past, Confucius himself was creative. There are times in history, and this was one of them, when to discredit the present in terms of the past is to herald a future like neither. And a disposition to revere the past can be an innovation in a society's intellectual life — something the past itself had scarcely known.

THE TRADITIONALIST

As a cure for the ills of his own society, Confucius urged the "rectification of names": a father should be a father, a minister should be a minister, a king should be a king. Confucius, we might say, is circular in his definitions — man is human, a son is filial. There is no true predicate.

This is characteristic of thinking in essences. One cannot say that a son has murdered his father, because it is essential that a son respect his father: *essential*, not in the sense that filial piety is binding on a son, but in the sense that he *is* not (he does not have the essence of) a son without it. A king does not starve or slaughter his people, because it is of the essence of kingship that a king brings harmony to the realm. If one fails in this and yet is called a king, that name must be "rectified." As the great Confucianist, Mencius, said, speaking of Shou Hsin, or Chou (the last ruler of Shang, that lengendary monster of evil), he knew no monarch, Chou — only a villain, Chou.

Now, an attribute of essence is eternity; *being* is by definition different from *becoming*. Kingship cannot change. Kings may change, but then they become "kings," usurpers of the name — and then title to the throne, *not* qualifications for the throne, should change. What Confucius sees is a world ideally of stasis, not process, because process, change, would be deviation from the original norm, the "Way," the *Tao*. The Tao is what is authentic and for all time; guilty men are inauthentic, wanderers from the Way. And one must not wander, must not move, for harmony, concord, the "real" state of the cosmos and society, is intrinsically the state of rest, and what dissolves rest into movement is discord. Confucius warned against "licentious music." When Confucius, as a moralist, deplores the discord of his own times and the inauthentic men who inspire it, he is disparaging movement and by implication the values of novelty or originality, for standards are fixed; if the present is wrong, then rightness must be in the past. The past provides man's good examples.

It also provides his bad examples. History, indeed (and history becomes the core of Confucianists' intellectual life), is conceived largely as a record of right and wrong conduct and their respective consequences. The historical emphasis is not on process but on incident. *History* has always meant the unfolding of narration for the European; time is its crucial element. Yet, the *shih* of the Chinese has its roots in time-less cosmology, in the immutable patterns that periodically reveal themselves, but only as the moon may on a cloudy night. When modern European ideas came to intrude on China, "history" came to be rendered by the binome *li-shih*. *Li* refers to the passing of time, but *shih* is obscure, for its original cosmological meanings have long since been forgotten.

Time does pass, of course. See the *Confucian Analects*

(*Lun-yü*, tr. James Legge) and the many commentaries —
but not all — which make it refer to "the things of time";
"The Master standing by a stream, said, 'It passes on just
like this, not ceasing day or night.' " "Change," after all, is a
classic term, and the condition of life, for the Confucianist.
But he strives, in his records of change (such as the record of
acknowledged process from legendary culture-hero kings, to
Golden Age, to the subsequent devolution), to identify and
promulgate the permanent.

The Confucian historian, then, with all his loving feeling
for detail, searches for eternal, archetypical situations; the
pastness of the past (the sense, with all its potentialities for
relativism, that the past is not present) and the *becoming-
ness* of the past (the sense that it is constantly dissolving
into the present) are not prominently savored. Confucius establishes this feeling for the paradigm in history, beyond
time, since his genius is for moral judgment, a type of absolute, and it necessarily resists the relativities of passing time
and change in the human condition. His *Spring and Autumn Annals of the State of Lu* (*Ch'un-ch'iu*) has always
been taken in Confucian circles as a historical framework
for moral and philosophical ideas. And the *Spring and Autumn* is at the bottom of the whole subsequent Confucian
historiographical enterprise. Ssu-ma Ch'ien's *Memoirs of the
Historian* (*Shih-chi*) was the prototype of the great omnibus
Dynastic Histories that cover the dynasties from Han to
Ch'ing; in the last chapter Ssu-ma declared that the aim of
his work was the same as that of the *Spring and Autumn*. In
the eleventh century Ssu-ma Kuang launched his significantly
entitled *Comprehensive Mirror for Aid in Government*
(*Tzu-chih t'ung-chien*), one of the most famous historical
works of all time, with the hope, redolent of the *Spring and
Autumn*, that "virtues might become examples and evils
warnings." In the seventeenth century another great scholar,
Ku Yen-wu, spoke of "using the Hsia and transforming barbarians", that is, invoking examples from a classical past as
still vital correctives for contemporary life. The reverence
for history as a storehouse of precedent and the interpretation of history from a standpoint of permanence (rather
than process) come together.

So much (for the moment) for history. If it is a treasury of moral examples, this is only an aspect of the fundamental Confucian injunction (traditionalist to the core) to "rule by example." As Confucius said in the *Analects* (*Lun-yü* tr. James Legge): "Let your evinced desires be for what is good, and the people will be good. The relation between superiors and inferiors, is like that between the wind and the grass. The grass must bend, when the wind blows across it."

Rule by example is traditionalist because it appeals (and this is the heart of Confucian moralism) to the inner quality of virtue, not to an outer system of laws and institutions. If men live under a system of impersonal laws they may, when things go badly, just change the system. But if virtue rules, one must change oneself, rectify oneself, and visible, outer change, the solvent of tradition, is discountenanced. At almost the end of Confucian history, in the 1890's, traditionalists accused the "Reformers" of that day of meaning to change the system (*fa*, the "laws": the compound for "reform" is *pien-fa*), thus violating the eternal Confucian injunction to look within to one's virtue (*te*) if the times demanded correcting. As George Orwell remarked (on the implications of the social thought of Dickens), a recommendation of change of heart is a classic move by conservatives to defend the *status quo*. Certainly the Chinese Confucian literati, who became the most prominent group in the empire, with a natural stake thereafter in resisting social change, found Confucius' emphasis on "virtue" (on *te-chih* over *fa-chih*, rule of virtue over rule of law) an appropriate commitment.

THE INNOVATOR

"Virtue" enshrined the old, then, not only in the sense that the virtuous sages were ancient and that moral decay implied the existence of primordial moral perfection, but also in the sense that "virtue" smothered the new: outer, visible tampering with the state of things, potentially novel action, was supposed to yield to inner self-correction and the consequent correction of the world by sympathy. *Nei sheng wai wang*, ran the Confucian formula — "Inside, sage; outside, king." The moral example of the harmonious soul commands the existence of harmony out in society.

But "old" is the opposite not only of "new" but of "young"; and Confucius' emphasis on virtue was a very significant counter to the values associated with youth. For Confucius, wisdom is very important, and one grows wise as one grows old. "The Master said, At fifteen I had my mind bent on learning. At thirty, I stood, firm. At forty, I had no doubts. At fifty, I knew the decrees of Heaven. At sixty, my ear was an obedient organ for the reception of truth. At seventy, I could follow what my heart desired, without transgressing what was right." (*Analects*, tr. James Legge.)

Those Were the Days: The Ideal Professor-Student Relationship. Confucius and his favorite disciple, Yen Tzu: "Sage walks, Yen follows." Korean printing, probably from worn Ch'ing blocks of late Ming works, *K'ung Fu-tzu sheng chi-t'u.*

Compare this with the tone of "The Scholars," by William Butler Yeats:

> Bald heads forgetful of their sins
> Old, learned, respectable bald heads
> Edit and annotate the lines
> That young men, tossing on their beds,
> Rhymed out in love's despair
> To flatter beauty's ignorant ear.

No Confucius, nor any Confucianist on duty (who might well be spending his respectable days editing and annotating), could have written this. It comes from another culture. The accent in Confucius' culture is on sobriety, not passion. There is little room for romanticism when youth is submerged by age.

That is why even poems from the Chou collection, the *Book of Songs (Shih-ching)*, which Confucius made a Classic — poems that to the modern non-Confucian eye are often transparently poems of youthful love — were encrusted over with sober, didactic interpretations in the Confucian tradition. What Arthur Waley renders as

> Out in the bushlands a creeper grows,
> The falling dew lies thick upon it.
> There was a man so lovely,
> Clear brow well rounded.
> By chance I came across him,
> And he let me have my will.

and Ezra Pound as

> Mid the bind-grass on the plain
> that the dew makes wet as rain
> I met by chance my clear-eyed man,
>   then my
>   joy began.

a Han dynasty Confucian text (second century B.C.) uses as a parable to hammer home the prosy point (allegedly in Confucius' words, tr. James Robert Hightower), "When a person does not transgress the boundary line in the great virtues, he may pass it and repass it in the small virtues." And for Confucius, who supposedly arranged this anthology, the *Book of Songs* as a whole was not what it seems to moderns, an outpouring of the popular muse. It was, instead, a political morality tale, expressions of emotion in such an order as to match the dynasty's fever chart — joy (for the early virtue), through gloom, to despair as virtue dims and the dynasty trembles. The poetry is history, good Confucian praise-and-blame history, concerned with process just to the extent that dynasties pass from light to dark, wax and wane, and set the stage for recurrence. The high seriousness of Confucianism converts the raptures of youth into the sage dicta of ancients.

Now, what does this overshadowing of youth by age portend? We know that Confucius, being a traditionalist, has to look back and praise the feudal system of early Chou, and this sounds, in our modern parlance, reactionary. Yet, it is precisely here, in his traditionalism, that Confucius shines forth as the innovator. *When traditionalism implies this exaltation of age over youth, do we not find some of the crucial values of feudalism denied?* Confucius defended feudalism, but he did so in terms that denied a basis of the feudal order: leadership through strength. *Ju*, the Confucian scholar, so highly placed in the impending imperial-bureaucratic society, had (in the still hypothetical etymology of the modern scholar, Hu Shih) the belittling connotation of "weakling" in its earliest usage.

A preference for age over youth means a preference for wisdom over brute martial vigor: war is mainly for the young. If the Confucian taste does not encompass the romance of youthful passion, neither does it encompass the romance of soldierly courage, a feudal value. As Max Weber noted, something important to the Chinese spirit was marked in the *Spring and Autumn Annals* when a prince was censured for listening to warriors, to youth, and not turning to the elders. It meant the virtual suppression of the epic strain in Confucian (the dominant) literature, for the courage of an epic hero was not the quality Confucianists preferred. In the *Book of Documents (Shu-ching)* as edited by Confucius, when a king wins out he is good and his foes are evil — there is none of the moral neutrality of the epic genre, where the generous recognition of an enemy's courage (transcending desire for long life) blurs the gray, essentially "elderly" judgments of moral right and wrong. Hector and Turnus, dying at the hands of Achilles and Aeneas in the greatest of Greek and Roman epics, are heroes, even though on the "wrong" side from the standpoint of the authors. By the values of medieval European chivalry, with its magnifying of feudal heroes to epic stature, the Muslim Saladin is a fair (though a dark!) counterpart of Richard the Lion-hearted. But Confucius and the Confucian tradition, far from such feudal values, never allowed such equivocation or moral ambiguity to invade their accounts of men and events.

Confucius, then, was a figure of grand paradox, an innovating traditionalist, harbinger of a future age that would clash with the past he ostensibly sought to revive. He was a Janus-headed figure, looking backward and forward: backward, because ideally, in the early Chou, behind feudal disintegration lay unity and stability — forward, because the only possible unity and stability for traditional China lay ahead of him, in the new postfeudal empire of the Ch'in and Han. His admiration for a past feudal order proved not so much an effectively positive attitude as a symbol of opposition to the present feudal disorder. For there can be more than one negation of any affirmation; and when he condemned contemporary chaos in the name of an antecedent order, he did so in the interests of a subsequent order, not the timelessly ideal but the historically possible one. It was a dialectical situation, like that of the men of the Renaissance and Reformation in Europe, who appealed respectively to ancient Hellenism and Gospel Christianity as preferred alternatives to some parts of their medieval inheritance, and in so doing heralded modern diversions from medieval values instead of reviving the old.

The old for Confucius was present in his words: *chün-tzu*, for example, a term from the feudal hierarchy, is ubiquitous in the *Analects*. But the new is present, too, the innovation in the traditional term. For Confucius characteristically moralized the term; its metaphorically new significance, as "princely man," "superior man," recalled the feudal order, but now suggested virtue and learning — both of them irrelevant to the feudal forms of hierarchy.

In short, when Confucius conjured up a splendid historical past, he was making a trenchant criticism of his own day and its inadequate ideas. His thought had a low content of romantic antiquarian dreaming. There was no brooding about decay in any passive, escapist fashion, no refuge in nostalgia. He never conveyed the pathos of a Don Quixote. Confucius' traditionalism was a philosophical principle rather than a psychological resting place — intellectually adaptable to a burgeoning society with a high degree of stability, not emotionally diversionary from his own society that was crumbling into ruin.

6

Background

"The Hundred Schools"

In the late Chou period, in the generations between the death of Confucius (479 B.C.) and the Ch'in unification of the empire (221 B.C.), there was a proliferation of contending schools of thought. Ssu-ma Ch'ien, in his Han master work, the *Shih-chi*, has left us Ssu-ma T'an's, his father's, pro-Taoist account that generalizes about these "hundred schools" under six main headings: *Yin-yang wu hsing chia* (Yin-yang five-elements school), *Ju-chia* (Confucianists), *Mo-chia* (Mohists), *Ming-chia* (Logicians), *Tao-te chia* (Taoists), *Fa-chia* (Legalists).

BRIEF IDENTIFICATIONS OF THE
MAJOR PHILOSOPHICAL SCHOOLS

Yin-yang five elements

Yin and yang are symbols of two correlative principles underlying the organization of the cosmos. Originally yang was "sun" and yin was "shadow"; they came to suggest other correlatives, like "male" and "female", and to relate to the connection between the human and cosmic orders. "Five elements" theory, originally independent, was ultimately bound up with yin-yang. The five elements — wood, fire, earth, metal, and water — succeed one another in an invariant cycle (just as the succession of yang and yin has an eternal rhythm), and each has a basic affinity for, or symbolic parallel in, a particular season, direction, color, virtue, physical organ, taste, plant, and domestic animal.

Confucianists

Mencius (372–289 B.C.) became known to Confucianists as the "Second Sage"; a great T'ang scholar, Han Yü (768–824 A.D.), named Mencius as the particular heir to Confucius' doctrine, and its last transmitter. Among the several moral qualities emphasized by Confucius, Mencius especially commended the "great four," *jen, i, li,* and *chih* — humankindness, propriety, ritual, and humane wisdom. Like Confucius, he stressed the importance of "rectification of names," and related this principle to the obligations of kingship. No true king could do other than care for the people's well-being; the people should be fed and clothed and spared the horrors of war. And the virtue essential to the true king was potential in every man — which is to say (a) that man is naturally good, a candidate (if he works hard) for sagehood, and (b) that monarchs may lose the "mandate of Heaven" which initially legitimizes their line, for, just as virtue may be anywhere, evil may come to the very point of the throne and make its holder the least of men instead of the greatest.

Hsün-tzu (315?–236? B.C.), making the external *li* nearer the center of his concerns than the internal *jen*, was, unlike Mencius, more concerned with social controls than rule by example; for Hsün-tzu, the nature of man was evil. To a greater extent than the intuitive Mencius, Hsün-tzu was a systematic reasoner, intent on approaching a formal presentation of Confucianism.

Two other "Ju" or Confucianists, Tseng-tzu and Tzu Ssu, flourishing after Confucius and before Mencius and Hsüntzu, were associated traditionally with the *Great Learning* (*Ta-hsüeh*); the name of Tzu Ssu, the grandson of Confucius, was also linked with the *Doctrine of the Mean* (*Chung-yung*). These Classics (both originally sections of the *Book of Rites*, the *Li-chi*), taken together, stress the subjective capacity and requirement for self-adjustment to the objective natural Way (*Tao*), the attainment by man of harmonious completeness in a cosmic-social continuum. And these Classics were indeed taken together, along with "Mencius" and the "Analects" (the *Lun-yü*, conversations of Confucius recorded by disciples), as the *Four Books*, established by the Sung philosopher, Chu Hsi (1130–1200 A.D.), as the heart of Confucian (or "neo-Confucian") education.

Mohists

Mo Ti, or Mo-tzu, who was active sometime between 479 and 381 B.C., was a particular target of Mencius' hostility. Mo-tzu's most important motifs were universal love, utilitarianism, and logic. Mencius concentrated his attack on the first of these, which implied the rejection of filial piety; Mencius paired Mo-tzu off with the Taoist individualist, Yang Chu, whose "each for himself" implied the rejection of loyalty to a monarch. Mencius: "To acknowledge neither prince nor father is to be one with the birds and beasts."

Mo-tzu fell even farther from Confucian grace since he justified universal love — itself unacceptable to Confucianists — by his utilitarian argument. Universal love meant mutual generosity, so that one could expect a fair return; one might not take special care of one's own parents, but some other universal lover would doubtless redress the lack, and ultimately the greatest number would profit. But "profit" — especially when its pursuit implied, as it did to Mo-tzu, the abandonment of frills like music and elaborate funerals — was anathema to Confucianists. And so was Mo-tzu's rejection of authority and precedent (those Confucian *sine qua non*), a rejection in favor of abstract reason as the tool for contriving order — whence the Mohist "Canons of Logic."

Part of the utility of universal love was supposed to be its contribution to inter-state peace. But in the short run the peace objective had to be sought, the Mohists said, by discouraging aggressors, and Mohists took very seriously questions of methods of warfare.

Logicians

The "Logicians," literally the "School of Names," seemed to take seriously the Confucian problem of "rectification of names," but they were thought to flout the Confucian concern for practical applicability. Such figures as Hui-tzu (380–300? B.C., known only through his contemporary critic, the Taoist, Chuang-tzu) and his disciple, Kung-sun Lung, aroused interest with their paradoxes and dialogues but were ultimately dismissed as purveyors of "empty words." The best-known contributions of this school are the essays on universals, "On a White Horse" and "On the Hard and the White," from the book known as the *Kung-sun Lung Tzu*. Here the almost ubiquitous philosophical problem of the relation between "reality" and the qualities accessible to sense perception finds one of its Chinese formulations.

Taoists

The Taoist classics identified with the pre-Ch'in period are *The Way and Its Power* (*Tao te ching*) and *Chuang Tzu*. They are "classics" only in the sense of being important repositories of certain conceptions. They never received (despite some ephemeral T'ang imperial sponsorship) the devoted protection, the official place in education, that the Confucian classics attained.

The *Tao te ching* is associated with the name of Li Erh, much better known as Lao Tzu. His birth date was traditionally set at 604 B.C., which does not correspond with the date of his book as we now have it. The *Tao te ching* (of "5000 words"), whose coherence and single authorship are hardly well established, was thought by modern scholars, by and large, to be a product of the first half of the third century B.C., but expert opinion now rejects this dating. Although Lao Tzu has been considered the *fons et origo* of Taoism, the *Chuang Tzu* book, the really compelling literary masterpiece of the Taoist school, has earlier material; it is basically fourth century B.C., with later admixtures. A third work, the *Lieh Tzu*, conventionally attributed to a sage mentioned in *Chuang Tzu*, was probably written as late as 300 A.D., near the time of the first basic commentaries on the *Tao te ching* and *Chuang Tzu*. "Spontaneity" (*tzu-jan*) is the basic concept. One of the *Lieh Tzu* chapters is given over to Yang Chu, the hedonist who was one of Mencius' *bêtes noires*.

As represented in these works, which are protean and

cryptic in varying degree, philosophical Taoism hymned a natural spontaneity, the participation of unselfconscious man in a single whole of life and death and the ground of being, the indefinable Tao, the Way. Indeed, any definition (most especially including the lines laid down by Confucian morality), any principle of separation, was anathema — whence the Taoist feeling of the relativity of all judgments. The texts abound in paradoxes that attempt (paradoxically) to express the inexpressible: for example, through nonactivity (*wu-wei*) all things may be done. (This is a key concept, politically, of a Taoist species of philosophical anarchism). "To cut without wounding" (or a myriad other similar paradoxical expressions): this is knowing the Way (but not by "knowing"). This is the Way that is always there, hidden to the timebound striver, open to the unthinking, undividing quietist, who is unridden by time, certain with the certainty of one who never seeks to ascertain. And there is the story of Chuang Tzu and the butterfly — one of the most famous parables in world literature. Chuang Tzu dreams he is a butterfly; awakens; *is* he Chuang Tzu who dreamt he was a butterfly; is he (equally unascertainable) a butterfly dreaming he is Chuang Tzu — or (the point, in the leaden prose of academics who try to make a point for Chuang Tzu), is there only a world of undifferentiated being, with no individuated subjects, no unambiguously predicated identities, no fixed landmarks and no points of view, only pulses that beat or wings that wave in the universal rhythm, only beings that move in Movement, and only by standing still?

Legalists

Legalism, a major influence from the fourth century B.C. (originating earlier, by a century or more) was a doctrine of harsh realism, pessimistic about the nature of man and the chances of order in a world entrusted to either Taoist *laisser faire* or Confucian moralism. Power was all, not virtue or knowledge, and the sovereign's power in a power state should be maximized. The major books in this tradition are the *Book of Lord Shang* (*Shang Chün shu*, early fourth century B.C.), *Kuan Tzu* (probably originating in the late fourth century B.C., edited and altered into its present corrupt form in Han times, attributed to a statesman of the seventh century B.C.), and *Han Fei Tzu* (attributed to Han Fei, d. 233 B.C.). Han Fei, synthesizing earlier Legalist theories, stressed both "art" and "law" — the ruler's manipulation of a public kept in the dark by his art in dissembling, and at the same time brought to clear awareness of his fixed law and stern punishments.

The Book of Lord Shang and *Kuan Tzu* emphasized the importance of agriculture. *Kuan Tzu* (which in certain ways is *sui generis*, not really fitting into the Legalist school) is an important though difficult text for economic history. It dwelled on the economic side of statecraft and avowed a realistic concern (unlike the Confucian scorn or condescension) for "profit." In the *Kuan Tzu* view of the world, a high (Confucian) moral tone was no substitute for — indeed, except as sham, it could hardly exist without — an economy of abundance.

Reading

Waley, Arthur, *Three Ways of Thought in Ancient China* (New York: Doubleday Anchor Books, 1965). Paperback (original edition 1939).

—— *The Analects of Confucius* (New York: Random House, 1960). Paperback (original edition 1938).

—— *The Way and Its Power: A study of the Tao Te Ching and its place in Chinese thought* (New York: Evergreen, 1958). Paperback (original edition 1934). See also Lau, D. C., *Lao Tzu: Tao Te Ching* (Harmondsworth: Penguin Books, 1963), paperback.

Watson, Burton, *Hsün Tzu: Basic Writings; Mo Tzu: Basic Writings; Chuang Tzu: Basic Writings; Han Fei Tzu: Basic Writings* (New York and London: Columbia University Press, 1963–1964). Paperbacks.

Wilhelm, Hellmut, *Change: Eight Lectures on the I Ching* (New York: Harper Torchbooks, 1964). Paperback (original edition 1960).

Implications

Disputation and Creativity

When Confucius, several centuries after his own time, finally became the sage *par excellence* of the Chinese intelligentsia, he testified to the intellectual vitality of late-Chou society, which had nurtured his genius. Did he testify also to a failure of vitality, Han and after, when his eminence, the very acknowledgement of his genius, presumably precluded any vigorous intellectual challenge? First, we must note that the presumption is shaky: as we shall see, Taoism and Buddhism openly, Legalism more covertly (i.e., without organization, without a coherent body of believers) continued to challenge Confucianism (as well as to affect it), and Confucianism itself developed various expressions. The presumption dates in China from the beginning of the twentieth century, when the "idea of progress" had entered the Chinese world and when Social Darwinism, conceiving of the progress as the fruit of struggle, became an important influence. Still, whatever the modern responsibility for the oversimplification of Confucian history, even from the standpoint of Han and post-Han Confucianists themselves late-Chou China was set apart, as an intellectual mother country, where their principles rose superior to alternatives in an atmosphere of polemical intensity.

What is the relation of disputation to vitality? Is it simply tautological to suggest any relation at all; are we just saying that where there is action there is life, and that disputation is action? Or may we see vitality precisely in the *result* of disputation, the fact that this controversy among the "Hundred Schools" established Confucianism's title to a long-sustained acceptance? Confucianism owed its long life to its character, and owed its character to the original conditions of combat.

Confucian*ism*, in intellectual character, was a "middle way." Confucian*ists*, as we shall see — principally that intelligentsia which became so intimately associated with bureaucracy in the post-Ch'in dynastic state — were, in social character, poised midway between aristocracy and autocracy.

We may well assume that the "middle" quality of Confucianism made it peculiarly fit for perpetuation, made it *vital*, in the impending long-lived bureaucratic society; and what was "middle" about Confucianism clearly emerges when we see it framed by sets of its late-Chou rivals.

All roads in Taoism pointed to egoism: the self was the Taoist's great concern — or, more literally, the banishment of self, the liberation and salvation of the ego from the fatal, death-directed consciousness of self. This banishment of self was not the Mohist banishment of self by the dictates of universal love; the latter was *altruistic*, not egoistic. Between these two lay Confucianism, with its injunction to "graded love," its feeling for specific, delimited human relationships that countered both the Mohist undiscriminating orientation out to all society and the Taoist quietist transcendence of any social attachments. Confucianism stood for the "near," midway between the Taoist individual "here" and the Mohist universal "far." It is in this sense that both Chinese family solidarity and Chinese cultural discrimination (not self, not world, but *family* and *culture*) became intimate parts of the typically Confucian world view.

But, more than Mohism, Legalism was the "outer," social extreme that paired with Taoism, the "inner," antisocial extreme, to set off Confucianism, the "inner-outer," compromising middle. The *Great Learning* (*Ta-hsüeh*) inextricably linked the concepts *hsiu-shen* (self-cultivation) and *p'ing t'ien-hsia* (world pacification), virtue of the individual and government of the collective. The Confucian ideal was establishment of social order among the governed by radiation of virtue from the governor. The Legalists, however, came down one-sidedly for "world pacification" (without the Confucian matching concern for self-cultivation) and for a social order, then, that owed everything to despotic power, exercised or menacingly held in reserve, and nothing to virtue, to a rule neither by force nor law but by example. And the Taoists (more specifically, Chuang Tzu), as philosophical anarchists, came down on the other, against government, against social order, for the primal virtue of a self tampered with neither by Legalist despotic manipulators nor by Confucian dispensers of that contrived, denaturing, *social* influence, education.

For the Taoists, nature, and *a fortiori* human nature, was good; hence education, an artificial gloss from the outside, could only be a blight on the natural. For the Legalists human nature was evil; hence only force could control it. But for the Confucianists human nature was good (the "Mencius strain," nearer to Taoism) and therefore *amenable* to education; or it was evil (the "Hsün-tzu strain," nearer to Legalism) and therefore *in need of* education. Either way, this Confucian ambiguity (corresponding to the inner-outer ambiguity, between Taoist "inner" and Legalist "outer") was yet another mediant affirmation, with education standing between the Taoists' blissful emptiness of mind and the Legalists' trust in force instead of learning.

The central ambiguity of the Confucian faith in education may perhaps be clarified by a modern analogy. Education, high culture, so peculiarly the Confucianists' concern and tied to that other Confucian concern, social order (guaranteed in the system of *li*, the ritual forms of "decorum"), had something of the air of a proto-Freudian value. Sigmund Freud (notably in *Civilization and Its Discontents*) saw the "socializing" force of education as involving the repression of instinctual gratifications, a "noble sacrifice of instinct," which inevitably engendered "discontents," but which also, through "sublimation" of potentially destructive instincts, made art and the higher forms of human expression possible. There was no hint in Confucian thinking of any psychic transformation, any *causal* nexus of social discipline and high culture, but the association of these two was there in Confucianism. It was not there in Taoism, for which the sacrifice of instinct could never be noble. And it was not there in Legalism, for which the sacrifice of instinct, the antisocial nature, was an end in itself, with no conversion of psychic energy into high culture, through sublimation, being conceivable as a by-product of the Legalist social controls.

The Taoist and Legalist poles have sometimes been said to come together, and in a sense they did, in their common egoism — despotic egoism of the solitary ruler (the one in the state) and anarchic egoism of the solitary hermit (the one in nature). The mechanical operation and the neutrality of the ruler's law had affinities with the Taoist ideal of noninterference, no tampering with the neutrality of nature. And this made for a common revulsion from the Confucian social and intellectual discipline, which was a restraint equally on anarchy and despotism. Whereas history was the perennial Confucian study and the appeal to history the favorite Confucian polemical device, Taoism and Legalism, straddling Confucianism, spurned history equally. For the Taoists, partisans of *wu-wei* ("nonactivity"), history was the weary story of action, man's impairment of the state of nature; for the Legalists, the appeal to history, that is, to precedent, was an unwelcome curb (as any curb would be unwelcome) on power, an impairment of the perfection of the ruler's freedom of action.

Indeed, the Legalist prescriptions were predominantly political, whereas the Taoist prescriptions, so thoroughly antipolitical, had, as a *constructive* force, predominantly cultural implications (though Taoism could lend itself, as we shall see, to political destructiveness). Confucianism was the golden mean in the sense that only Confucianism was ecumenical. Its ideas pervaded both the realm of government (as the Legalist did) and the realm of the imagination (as the Taoist did) — which is only to say that Confucianism broke down the isolation of the separate schools and made them, in any pure sense, hypothetical. We shall see how Confucianism and Legalism together made political China in the bureaucratic-imperial postclassical regimes, and how Confucianism and Taoism together (with Buddhism still to come) made cultural China. The common term, the middle way, the fulcrum for the balance that stability implies, was *Confucianism*.

What was stability but the power to survive, that power which is vitality? It seems rather a romantic foible of historians to attribute "health" to the period of quest and struggle, with achievement and victory written off as fatal infections. The real culture paradox, the real value problem about cultural efflorescence is yet to be formulated: not, "Is war the health of the cultural state?" ("Is victory defeat?"), but, "What system of values can reconcile cultural efflorescence with concomitant social disaster?" For men do judge, no matter how single-mindedly (and chimerically), as historians, they may direct their researches to "how it really was." We shall defer the problem of judgment until we come, first, to the breakdown of T'ang.

Background

The "Warring States" (403-221 B.C.) and Ch'in (221-206 B.C.)

THE MILITARY RESOLUTION OF THE
PROBLEM OF DISUNITY

Ch'in, which ultimately liquidated Chou feudalism and established the new centralized imperial system, was still politically insignificant in the "Spring and Autumn" period and down through the fifth century B.C. It was not one of the "Six States" that were initially the main characters in the drama of the "Warring States". Facing barbarians on the northwest marches of the Chinese world (in the area of the modern provinces of Shensi and Kansu), Ch'in was considered at least half-barbarian itself by the inner states, and "the Six" never put together an effective alliance against it. One of their own number, Ch'u, in the south (i.e. in modern Hunan, Kiangsi, and Szechwan), came to seem to the others the greatest threat, and, even when Ch'u was flagging, the zeal to combine against it clouded their recognition of Ch'in as the rolling, crushing chariot of conquest. An alliance of sorts was pasted together in 333 B.C., but it was only a moment of truth, and disunited states, one by one down to 221 B.C., vanished into the Ch'in holdings.

The original Western Chou enfeoffment, by various early counts (e.g. *Tso-chuan, Shih-chi*) engendered from 70 to 90 feudal states, of which two-thirds were of the royal Chou surname (Chi). Subinfeudation ensued, and some hundreds of fiefs existed at the start of the "Spring and Autumn" period. But the number had boiled down to ten by the fourth century, and finally down to the big one. Whatever unity there once had been, however close it was to the Confucian ideal of a great chain of moral links, internecine warfare had dissolved it; the Chou center could not hold. Unity was reconstituted by Ch'in, but emphatically not through morality, and the new, actual unity was not the feudal ideal. Unity now was that of a society with a new cultural, economic, and political character, a bureaucratic society — based on a centralized state, which was staffed by a literate bureaucracy, whose power derived from a combination of interests in land and office.

SOCIAL CONCOMITANTS OF THE POLITICAL UPHEAVAL

The Ch'in brand of warfare, which put an end to the political existence of the "Warring States," had already subverted the social basis of their feudal polity. Earlier in the Chou period and back into Shang, warfare had been almost an aristocratic preserve, with nobles in chariots dominating hostilities. Then, much later, by the fifth or fourth century B.C., pettier nobles on horses held the field. It was in Ch'in, precisely where the public power of the state first encroached upon the private power of nobles, that peasants began to be soldiers, no longer merely escorts and servants in war. The aristocratic honor of the profession of arms was thus diluted, and the associated aristocratic honor of land tenure (accorded to lords for service to suzerain, and inaccessible to peasants merely working the land, like European villeins) began to lose its basis. Ch'in peasants (as well as those of the larger states generally) gained rights of possession, just as Ch'in peasants flooded the new army — which helped to liquidate feudalism at home, in Ch'in, by their presence, and abroad, in what would become Ch'in, by the power they brought to bear. As Ch'in conquered new lands, their administration was handed over to centrally appointed state officials, not to aristocratic, anticentral acquirers of fiefs.

The forces that Ch'in channelized to destroy feudalism were not peculiar to Ch'in. Population was growing everywhere, spurred by such innovations as the use of iron, which considerably improved the technology of agriculture: in plowing, for example. The means of transportation improved, too, facilitating the trade relations that began to form and to link new burgeoning urban districts. This process made it harder (as in late feudal Europe) to pin people to servile status on the land.

Indeed, the land needed more than the application of animal-drawn plows to begin to support the population. War might thin them out, and the "Warring States" obliged. But irrigation and flood control could help to sustain them, and control of water (by projects like building dikes to check the Yellow River, with its rising bed and menace of drift in new directions) became absolutely mandatory. And here a centralized state's ability to marshal power was virtually indispensable; for labor had to be mobilized in vast numbers, and a state apparatus called into being to supervise the task, and to collect the resources for supporting that effort — and supporting itself. It should occasion no surprise that in the *Institutes of Chou (Chou-li)*, the one Classic almost invariably invoked by the strongest centralizers throughout imperial Chinese history, the Ministry of Public Works, theoretically responsible for the control and exploitation of water, was reserved for the Chou ruling family. The facts of Chou, of course, were progressive decentralization, but the *Institutes of Chou*, essentially late and spurious as history, was a fair guide to some new values emerging from the Chou debacle.

The ultimate aim was the creation of a powerful state in which the masses would be contented and order maintained by a single powerful ruler. The duty of the king's ministers would lie in constantly strengthening the central authority, keeping vigilance over the society to prevent hostile movements from arising. In such a state, there would be no classes. There was no room for an aristocracy that would demand to share power with the ruler. The feudal aristocracy had been the cause of conflict. In the process of forming the new state, the aristocrats were to be eliminated. Distinctions of rank would remain between those who exercised command and those who obeyed. But the titled bureaucrat was meant to be simply the servant of the monarch, his tool in creating and maintaining order. There was thus not to be any element in society to wield power between ruler and subject.

Of all the going systems of ideas, the strongly statist Legalism was most in tune with these times. The state of Ch'i (in modern Shantung) had anticipated even Ch'in in the use of iron and was prominent as a state producer of salt. This was noteworthy for two reasons: trade in salt and iron, in the coming imperial China, became the hardiest of perennial state monopolies, significant for and symbolic of the pretensions of the state — and Kuan Tzu, known (anachronistically) as a Legalist, was the state of Ch'i's most distinguished intellectual figure. But Ch'in outstripped Ch'i's Legalist effort, and the Ch'in minister, Kung-sun Yang or Shang Yang, the "Lord of Shang," made a much greater mark than Kuan Tzu on the history of the "Warring States" and after.

As a centralizer, Shang Yang had more promising material to work with. For not only droughts or floods of water were constant threats to the social peace of China, but floods of barbarians, and Ch'in had taken a major part in barbarian control. This, too, was a stimulus to state effort, the bureaucratic organization of labor. At the turn of the fourth and third centuries, Ch'in as one of the "Warring States" built an antinomad wall (though not the first: other states had built walls already), which became a building-block for the Great Wall, that fantastic project, decades later, of Ch'in as the ruler of empire. Shang Yang had already been on the scene.

The Legalist rigor of Shang Yang (who was finally executed, torn to pieces for his pains) was felt in Ch'in during the years 361–330 B.C. While his patron, Duke Hsiao, lived, Shang Yang was able to make his assault on feudal distinctions. Generally applicable penal law, standardization of weights and measures and the like had their part, but it was new policy on the land that had the broadest anti-feudal ramifications. Primogeniture was ended (lastingly, only from Han times, second century B.C.) — which meant that land became *divisible* among heirs, diffusing the power of private individuals *vis-à-vis* the state; and it meant that land became *alienable* to the general public, became a commodity, open to all comers. In the standard Confucian accounts, these are the developments alluded to under the guise of "Shang Yang's liquidation of the well-field (*ching-t'ien*) system."

The "well-field system" was described by Mencius and remained an ideal of social harmony for all subsequent Confucianists — even for those, like Chu Hsi (1130–1200 A.D.), who held it to be unviable in their own unsagely times — and an inspiration for certain modern socialists. The name derived from the character *ching* 井 (well), a suggestive model-to-scale of a nine-square plot (three *li* by three *li* in all), with eight families farming their own squares for themselves and the central square in common for the lord, the public authority. Though doubtless no system as schematic and universal as Mencius' ever existed, his "well-field" description (and certain other Classical references) may well be reminiscences of an early system of land utilization in common, with a lord above his peasants and sustained by them. In any case, manorial property had developed, and what Confucianists called the Ch'in attack on *ching-t'ien* we must call the Ch'in attack on feudal decentralization. What Ch'in was doing was establishing the free right of buying and selling land (which indeed would be subversive of a hypothetical *ching-t'ien* system of regular, fixed allotments). This meant that Ch'in spread its vital power to tax throughout its domain, and bequeathed this ideal to subsequent dynasties.

As Ch'in spread its domain throughout the empire, Legalist measures continued to be taken and extended. The Ch'in king who came to the throne in 246 B.C. became the "Fist Emperor," Ch'in Shih Huang-ti, in 221 B.C. (d. 210 B.C.). As a man of rage, impetuosity, even megalomania, he was ready enough to strive for the Legalist goal of power; he was well served by ministers who supplied what he lacked, the Legalist style of impersonal rationality. Lü Pu-wei, a merchant (deposed from power in 237 B.C., suicide in 235 B.C.) was succeeded in influence by Li Ssu (280?–208 B.C.), and standardization in many fields — laws, script, coinage, weights, measures — ensued. Shang Yang's old assault on feudalism was consummated, with the whole empire divided into thirty-six commanderies, staffed by appointment from the center, as feudal political influence was utterly reduced. To make an end of feudal military influence, weapons were wrested from private hands, as the state sought a monopoly of military power. And books were collected, too, especially the Classics of the Confucianists who persisted in citing antiquity to shame the present. Li Ssu procured the burning of the books in 213 B.C.; Confucian records of historical tradition, he insisted, should not be allowed to shadow the pure light of Legalist abstraction.

It was the Emperor himself who in 212 B.C. initiated the project of "burying the scholars" (some four hundred), a mad assault on Confucianists (among others), to complement the reasoned proscription of Confucian ideas. Ch'in had established the empire, and *raison d'état*, "reason of state," made it antifeudal and (initially) anti-Confucian: the Legalist state conflicted with feudal estates, and Legalist reason conflicted with the Confucian devotion to history.

Reading

Hsu Cho-yün, *Ancient China in Transition: an Analysis of Social Mobility*, 722–222 B.C. (Stanford: Stanford University Press, 1968). Paperback (original edition 1965).

Implications

The Problem of Historical Analogy: (b) Feudalism as Stage

"Feudalism", for all the refinements of definition that historians are making, and the variant forms they discern and qualify, is a single name, an abstraction from some of the political and social and economic facts of medieval European history. Yet, we have imposed it blithely already on the facts of Chou history. Did the reader stop to consider then what tremendous assumptions were being made? A name, a universal, induced from particular things (*European*), was being brought down to things (*Chinese*) that had developed independently of the world of the induction. Does this imply a judgment that histories are uniform, that, in this case, long centuries of Chinese and European histories could have been really interchangeable? Or does the use of the European term "feudalism" present a case not of objective *historical analogy* but of subjective *historian's comparison*, to the end of clarifying the individualities of Chinese and European histories, not their sameness? Typologies of history, like Spengler's and Toynbee's, assume a morphological uniformity, parallel life cycles of civilizations, and Marxists, too (certainly Chinese Marxists, as we have suggested in connection with the problem of Shang "slave society"), find in history a principle of universal development. What is the difference between such assumptions of uniformity in the various historical records and an assumption that a principle for explaining *one* history — if it really explains, really establishes some unity among manifold data — has a part to play, as a point of theoretical departure, in explaining other and dissimilar ones?

We begin, then, with the acknowledgment that feudalism is a name a historian attaches first to a combination of things from an *individual* history, for example, the history of Western Europe: one must start somewhere, and starting with Europe has only a heuristic significance, no normative significance whatever. But the combination deserves a name only so far as the things seem appropriate to one another, making a little world, not just a chance association. The more inclusively and complexly any other individual history (such as Chou history or a part of Japanese history) seems to yield a like combination, the more conclusively the historian possesses a world of data and no mere association. He has grounds for assuming that certain things *belong together* in history — such things as the private possession of political authority and primogeniture in the system of inheritance, inhibiting the free disposition of land. "Belonging together" does not imply that one of these elements in the combination cannot exist in history without the other. "Belonging together" implies, rather, that if the term "feudalism" is being correctly applied, certain characteristics must be present jointly.

What redeems this from being semantic haggling is the fact that the world of data in feudalism, the necessary ingredients in the combination, are both static and dynamic. Feudalism has both system and process — its typical institutions and values, on the one hand, and tendencies, on the other. Facts about where it is going are some of the facts that reveal what it is. Accordingly, what a historian may be seeking if he tests a society for feudalism is not the sheer joy of label-pinning but the perception of one of the label's implications: that capitalism is on the way. Thus, the distinction between post-Chou, non-feudal imperial China and feudal medieval Japan may be invoked to throw light on the comparatively easy emergence of Japan into the modern capitalistic world.

It is just here that the distinction becomes important between actual repetition of a system in different histories, and applicability of the *concept* of the system to analysis of different histories. If, judging from European history and strengthening the judgment with a Japanese parallel, we conclude that one of the characteristics of feudalism is its forming a matrix for the evolution of capitalism, then — as long as we look for actual historical analogy — Chou China, for all its "static" affinities with foreign feudal systems, seems to lack the dynamic that would establish the analogy. For Chou China evolved into a Confucian bureaucratic society that diverged from capitalism on many points. Should we try, then, to save the Chou for feudalism by paring down the list of characteristics in the feudal combination, eliminating the item of culmination in capitalism? Should we try the opposite expedient, saving feudalism for the Chou by admitting all sorts of variations in characteristics to shelter under the same heading? But what is the good of preserving, by any expedient, an abstraction from history at the cost of dismissing the raw historical problems to which it ought to be relevant? What we need to see is, not Chou China safely pigeon-holed as feudal, just like medieval Europe, but Chou China as feudal *enough* to identify a crucial question about it: what kept it from realizing the full implications of feudalism in the European sense?

If we define feudalism so as to make the origins of capitalism relevant, and if we view Chou China as feudal enough, on so many counts, that capitalist development should theoretically be expected, then the application here of the idea of feudalism points up the question. What are the forces inhibiting Chinese capitalism even while an ostensibly feudal, hence potentially capitalist society evolves into something antifeudal — something, but not the capitalism that comes in the western sequence? Or, to give the question a positive twist — why does a hypothetical feudalism yield to a bureaucratic society, which is not only antifeudal but anticapitalist as well? The feudal hypothesis explains so much of Chou China that one is prompted to ask why it does not explain the whole.

Measured against the western idea of feudalism, the undeniable qualitative change between pre-Ch'in and post-Ch'in society can be seen as transition to an antifeudal society, from a society *incompletely* analogous to the European feudal one. The inception of the post-Ch'in antifeudalism, since it is also anticapitalist — a continuing depressant of capitalism, in fact — comprises the incompleteness of the analogy. The Confucianism of imperial bureaucratic China seems equidistant from Chou feudalism and modern capitalism, and the feudal ideal type, helping us to define by contrast both the static and dynamic qualities of Confucianism, both its structure and its conduciveness to change, is the key to comprehension of this Confucian mean position.

We have suggested that Confucian intellectuality ran counter to the feudal admiration of the soldier's virtues. Confucian opposition to a chivalric code of heroes was a turn to the elders, to learning over courage, and to a system of examination of learning (adumbrated in Han, consolidated in T'ang) as the ideal road to power and prestige, circumventing those juridical guarantees of status that feudalism accorded to birth. And the examinations stressed a *traditional* learning, not original thought, because age over youth meant not only counsellor over warrior but old over new: the rule of precedent, the rule of example.

Such a reverence for precedent may sound close to feudalism, but feudal spokesmen, as we know from the European experience, dwelt extensively on tradition only when feudalism was coming to be obsolete and under fire. Actually, Confucianism was separated from feudalism, not linked to it, by precedent-seeking, since Confucian traditionalism, although it assumed that virtue could be expressed in objective norms, was based on rejection of *fa-chih*, the rule of law (a contrived system which man may change), in favor of *te-chih*, the rule of virtue, radiated by example. Confucian society was meant to be a stable moral network — hence pinned to prior-existing truths, so that change of heart must always preclude change of system — not a precarious legal network, like feudalism. The fact that Confucian social ideals purported to express the original vision of a dying feudal society does not preclude our making this distinction. For Confucian ideals reflected social change — and intellectual change to traditionalism as an anchor that would drag against change — by cherishing an old, feudal vocabulary while charging it with new connotations.

The affinity of feudalism with capitalism, which Confucianism lacks, is here, in their common dependence on law and contract. Max Weber was anxious to make a negative proof of his famous Protestant-ethic-to-European-capitalism thesis, by showing the quite non-Protestant Confucian ethic as the inhibitor of otherwise probable capitalism in China. He assumed that in the long centuries of prominence of the Confucian ethic Chinese society was more strongly proto-capitalist than European feudal society. He did this by failing to stress the continuity of contractual legalism in European history and concentrating on such things as the apparently common cause that modern capitalist and imperial Chinese society, beginning with Ch'in, pressed against feudal primogeniture. But the cause is not common. Rather, feudalism has the closer tie to capitalism, since, in both, the legal identification of person with property was established; feudal class-freeze and property-freeze had only to be swept away, by the revolution they provoked, for capitalist individualism to grow. But in imperial China the principle of anti-primogeniture was part of a system of familial communalism which, while anti-feudal enough (feudalism being based more on contract than on kinship), consistently blocked that identification of property with person so essential to capitalism, to capitalist requirements of clear-cut, unequivocal, multiple, and rapid commercial decisions. And revolution, which might have removed *that* anticapitalist block in China, was historically aborted by the antifeudal, relatively free, traditional social mobility that ideally comes so close to a capitalist characteristic.

The high degree of stability which this account suggests for Chinese society in the Confucian period, that long interval between feudalism (or what would have been feudalism unequivocally if the interval had not occurred) and capitalism, an interval that Japanese history missed, was intellectually captured in the Chinese examination idea — antifeudal in conception and anticapitalist in effect. The Japanese had shuffled it off as they moved irrevocably into a feudal age from a T'ang-inspired would-be bureaucratic one, and feudalism never cast the spell that the examination-ridden Confucian society did against capitalist modernism or antitraditionalism and new ideas from the modern western capitalistic world. For nineteenth-century Japanese leaders, whose feudal origins made their status rest on assumptions of birth rather than on assumptions of possession of a given corpus of knowledge, had a greater intellectual flexibility than Chinese literati, the heirs of antifeudal ages.

Why were these ages antifeudal? It is significant that in late-Chou China, where the dissolution of feudalism was well on its way on its own, the conscious liquidation of feudal institutions was directed by *state authority*, notably (though not exclusively and not as the first) in the once-feudal conquest state of Ch'in. This is an indication that centrally directed bureaucratic action was perhaps the *sine qua non* of a viable social order. This is far from saying that such bureaucratic action always effectively existed; it implies only that, in the last analysis, would-be feudal power in China could not be power, for the world it ruled would be too distressed and disturbed to support any stable base of power. A feudal system of private (aristocratic) exploitation of land withdrawn from the reach of the state was one thing. But recurrent *bureaucratic* exploitation of an antifeudal state power was another — and more viable, more lucrative. It led, recurrently — *without* proceeding by feudal stage to capitalism — in a feudal direction. But if it was not capitalist, it was only *feudalizing*, not feudal. After Chou, China was only abortively feudal, occasionally: a reconstituted imperial-bureaucratic state was a sounder generator of power for men at the top than any feudal-supremacy system that men at the top might staff.

With the end of Chou in the clash of warring states, the groundwork was laid for bureaucracy to succeed feudal aristocracy as the status group most prominently sharing and contesting power and position with the throne. This bureaucracy became — not immediately but inexorably, not completely but predominantly — associated with Confucianism, and, to say the same thing, this bureaucracy was not a capitalist class. Land and office and intellectual prestige primarily, commerce and finance only secondarily and indirectly, manufacturing never until the end, formed the basis of its power. We shall soon discuss the (ambiguous) dependence of these Confucianists on the centralized dynastic state, a link forged in the common experience of Confucianism and monarchy in setting feudal China to rest.

We call it a *feudal* China, after all, because the analogy of the *system* with feudal Europe's is strongly suggested — so strongly, in fact, that the capitalism implied as the end product of the feudal *stage* must lurk in the historian's mind, if not on the Chinese historical scene. And we, as historians, will then see the importance of things unseen in the record: we will see the reality, not just of what occurred, but of the nonoccurrence of some things that we plausibly might expect. We will discern, that is, in the Confucian-colored, Legalist-shaped, bureaucratic-imperial post-feudal system, the qualities of inhibitor of capitalism, a capitalism that would have obtained if the insistently potential feudal analogy were actually perfect.

In short, attribution of feudalism to the Chou is not ruled out by the noncapitalist quality of its successor age. For the feudal dynamic toward capitalism may be assumed to be present — pressure for capitalism in pre-Ch'in — since post-Ch'in has so much the character of *repressor* of capitalism. As such, it casts light back on the Chou as feudal. And the Chou as feudal casts light ahead on a Ch'in-Han and subsequent China, which can never be sufficiently explained as merely antifeudal. *Confucian* China must be seen as anticapitalist, a depressant of capitalism, as well.

Background

From Ch'in to Han: I, Confucianists and Office

LEGALIST POWER

Chinese scholars of later ages have always viewed the Ch'in dynasty with extreme distaste. The image of Ch'in Shih Huang-ti as a usurper, murderer, burner of books, oppressor of the masses has remained as firmly embedded in China as the image of Nero has remained in the West. To some extent, the hatred of China's "first emperor" stems from the fact that he was the one who snapped the thread to the golden age of antiquity. Subsequent generations of writers always thought longingly of the "three dynasties," and it was felt either that a golden age might one day reappear, or that at least it remained as a standard and model, a perennial ideal.

But it was perhaps not so much Ch'in Shih Huang-ti's role as revolutionary and innovator that appalled men, as the manner of his rule and the nature of the order that he attempted to establish. After all, the period of the Warring States was one of great chaos, and no Chinese literatus ever yearned for a return to such times. Moreover, it would have to be to his credit that Ch'in Shih Huang-ti established a system of unified government upon which two thousand years of Chinese political tradition were based. As unifier of China he could not be attacked without calling into question the system under which later Confucianists lived and acted. What repelled them most about him was something else. The literati of China always had a great fear of power — power that left some men at the mercy of others and that could arbitrarily destroy them physically or socially. Ch'in Shih Huang-ti ruled his great realm through naked power.

The old authority had disappeared, but the new system of control had not yet been legitimized. Ch'in Shih Huang-ti had proclaimed himself emperor of China, yet there were many in the country who did not accept him as such. As long as his forceful personality reigned, as success followed success, and as his armies and bureaucrats kept a tight grip on the empire, men would obey. But they obeyed out of fear, not conviction. The image of Ch'in Shih Huang-ti that has persisted is that of the despot ruling through power and not authority. Though men of power (physical, martial power, even without concomitant political power) have fascinated the common people of China — witness the adoration of the deified warrior, Kuan Yü, in Taoist temples, or the admiration of the other contending captains of the San Kuo ("Three Kingdoms") period — the literati, by and large, always feared power. Given the political system of centralization, great power could only mean power at the very top. Powerful emperors surrounded by power-hungry sycophants, imperial relatives, eunuchs, wives, and concubines could only spell evil times for the literati officials. The literati demanded a rule of authority based on mutual acceptance of common values. This Ch'in Shih Huang-ti was unable to bring about.

Power is always hard to institutionalize. When power is bound up with a single great man, the dilemma created by his demise is particularly acute. Lesser men begin to struggle for power and often succeed in blunting its effectiveness. Where a society is ruled by power alone and regular authority is weakly established, a time of danger has come. This happened to the Ch'in after the death of Ch'in Shih Huang-ti in 210 B.C. The succession to the new imperial throne was unclear. A classical account states that Ch'in Shih Huang-ti had designated his eldest son, Fu Su, as his

A JAPANESE VERSION OF CONFUCIUS

By Tosa Mitsuoki (1617-1691). Original in color.
See *Kokka*, No. 440 (July 1927).

THE DRAGON SCROLL

by Ch'en Jung, thirteenth century
(Museum of Fine Arts, Boston)

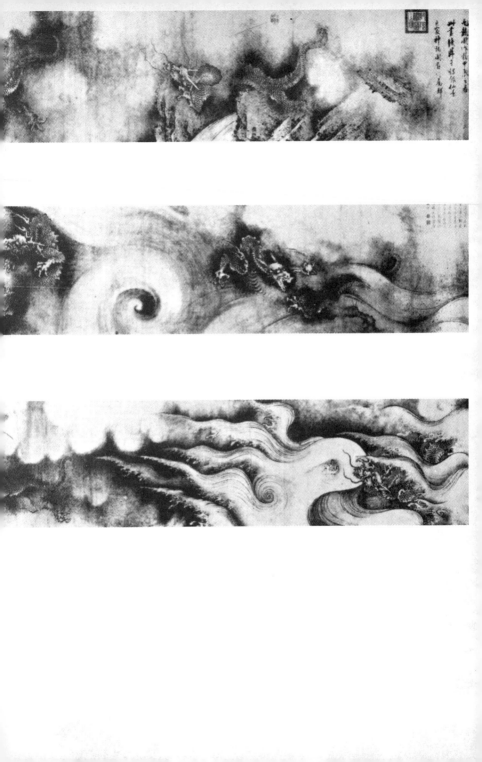

successor, but that the machinations of the chief minister, Li Ssu, and the eunuch, Chao Kao, succeeded in putting a younger son, Hu Hai, on the throne as Erh Shih Huang-ti or second emperor. Other scholars believe that Ch'in Shih Huang-ti never intended turning over the throne to his eldest son. The important fact is that, whatever the mechanisms for succession and the will of the emperor, both failed to avert that struggle for power which in a few short years led to the collapse of the Ch'in dynasty. Frustration led to killing. Those who grasped for power, Hu Hai, Chao Kao, and Li Ssu, were all killed.

The collapse at the top let loose all the resentments that had been growing during Ch'in Shih Huang-ti's rule. Scions of the old aristocracy, the oppressed peasantry, and the intellectuals rose up against a regime whose authority they did not recognize. In Wu (now the Shanghai region), Hsiang Liang and his nephew, Hsiang Yü, descendants of an old family of Ch'u, mobilized armies and marched westward along the Yangtze River. In all the provinces the common people rose and killed the Ch'in officials. Local rulers under the traditional title of king (*wang*) asserted themselves against the central power, what little there was left of it. Hsiang Liang set up his own King of Ch'u. In the north, a King of Chao appeared. In Hopei, Liu Pang, the future first emperor of the Han, organized an army and joined the struggle against the Ch'in armies.

Hsiang Yü again and again routed the remnant Ch'in armies. In the Ch'in capital, desperation reigned. Chao Kao killed the second emperor and set up a new emperor, Ying, the grandson of Ch'in Shih Huang-ti. But the new emperor killed his king maker, only to surrender soon to the armies of Liu Pang in Ch'ang-an district. In 206 B.C. the Ch'in dynasty disappeared forever.

But the triumph of Liu Pang (or Liu Chi), unlike that of Ch'in Shih Huang-ti, was not absolute. Great armies under the command of Hsiang Yü faced him. The people who had revolted against despotism were not inclined to see the reestablishment of despotism. The mood was for compromise and, perhaps more important, restoration. Hsiang Yü demanded that the old feudal system be reestablished and that the King of Ch'u be made into an emperor of merely symbolic authority. The descendants of the rulers of the "six kingdoms" and the men of merit in the Ch'in were to receive fiefs. Power was to remain dispersed in the hands of military chiefs like Hsiang Yü and Liu Pang. Liu Pang accepted these proposals, then broke the compact soon, and attacked and destroyed Hsiang Yü.

But again his triumph was not absolute. Liu Pang won as the commander in chief of an alliance of local warlords and armies. Though he was offered and accepted the title of emperor, he recognized that he could not rule with absolute power. Power had to be shared with those who had helped him to victory. These were the kings of Ch'u, Liang, Chao, Han, Huai-nan, Yen, and Ch'ang-sha. Liu Pang destroyed these rivals in turn and made himself sole master. However, in the process he needed the aid of his relatives, who commanded armies and fought his enemies. Again he had to compromise. In place of the old traditional kings, members of the house of Liu received their enfeoffments. True, as time wore on their span of control diminished and that of the central authority increased. However, the principle of shared authority had been established. Liu Pang ascended the throne as emperor but not as despot. A mediating structure designed to check the tendencies toward absolute power had been set up. Later on, as it happened, it was the bureaucracy that shared authority, not the new feudatories. But the principle of central power tempered by mediation, through some body of sharers, had won out. It was on this foundation that the Han dynasty and all later dynasties were set up.

THE "ESTABLISHMENT" OF CONFUCIANISM

Confucianists succeeded aristocrats as the sharers of power when bureaucracy, in the public sphere, once more enabled the state to withhold power from private spheres. Bureaucracy became *Confucian* — that is, became the characteristic, sought-out haven of Confucianists, while Confucian learning and officials' status gained the highest prestige, intellectual and social, respectively — when the monarch acknowledged that it cost him something to vanquish his noble rivals: all the power thus regained could not accrue to him.

He had to share with his bureaucracy, as the Ch'in had not shared. The Ch'in tyranny, with its famous anti-Confucian (and generally anti-anti-Legalist) features of the "burning of the books" (213 B.C.) and the "burial of the scholars" (212 B.C.), its Legalist hatred of the "study of the past to belittle the present," was simply not viable. The Confucian penchant for books and traditions, with the restraints they implied on absolute autocracy, had to be allowed to redeem the lives of its bureaucratic servants. Autocracy had to be muted if it was ever to be really served.

Thus, it was under Emperor Wu of Han (Han Wu-ti, regn. 140–87 B.C.), the most vigorous and successful of all successors of Liu Pang, that Confucianism became intellectually the dominant creed and socially the best-connected one. Wu appointed scholars to high places in government, endorsed the tenet of "wisdom through the study of the Classics" by establishing schools, and limited study in the schools to the Confucian canon. For higher education, a Confucian college was founded with five faculties, each specializing in one of the canonical Classics (*Changes, Documents, Odes, Rites*, and *Spring-and-Autumn Annals*). A rudimentary examination system for entrance into the civil service was established (only T'ang really institutionalized this, in the seventh century A.D.); it tested ability to read the Classics, since the language in official documents was patterned after them. Ssu-ma Ch'ien, writing ca. 100 B.C., describes this period as one in which increasing numbers of scholars were being employed as ministers, high officials, and magistrates. Tung Chung-shu, who saw the Classics as augur books where bureaucrats should read cause-and-effect into sequences of political and natural phenomena, gave the decisive advice (recorded in the *Ch'ien Han shu,* [*History of the Former Han Dynasty,*] the first successor to Ssu-ma Ch'ien's *Shih-chi*): "Reinforce education. When education is well established, the ruler and his descendants will be prosperous . . . establish an imperial academy. . . . Give examinations in order to select the best."

Tung Chung-shu also gave economic advice. We shall soon see what bearing this had on the relationship between bureaucracy and monarchy.

Reading

Bodde, Derk, *China's First Unifier: A Study of the Ch'in Dynasty as Seen in the Life of Li Ssu, 280:–208* B.C. (Hong Kong: Hong Kong University Press, 1967; original edition 1938).

Watson, Burton, *Records of the Grand Historian of China: translated from the Shih Chi of Ssu-ma Ch'ien* (New York: Columbia University Press, 1961).

Dubs, Homer H., *The History of the Former Han Dynasty by Pan Ku* (Baltimore: Waverly Press, 1938, 1949), Vols. I, II.

Implications

Bureaucracy, Monarchy, and Social Stability: Confucianism and Legalism as Political Correlatives

In Communist China, the term *Han* is used to designate Chinese, as opposed to Mongols, Uighurs, Tibetans, and other minorities, whereas the term *Chung-kuo-jen* (literally, man of China) covers them all in the sense that all are inhabitants of the territory of China. Why should a single dynasty (or two-in-one), a historical period, give a generic name to a people who went through many dynastic periods? This is not usual in world history, and it tells us something about the staying-power of Chinese social arrangements. And why should it be particularly Han — not Hsia, Shang, and Chou, the dynasties of which the Confucian Classics speak — that thus transcends the others? "Hsia" *has* had some currency in some parts of China because the Han Confucian establishment diffused so well the legend of Hsia as seminal. And "T'ang" has had some currency, too, in southeast China — because it was the T'ang dynasty (618–906

A.D.) that firmly bound these areas into the state and cultural system that Han had adumbrated. It was only "Han" that transcended region and became the mark of the basic, proliferating branch of the people of all China.

Hsia, Shang, and Chou have their own transcendence; for the "sons of Han" they became the *san-tai*, the "three dynasties," the classical ages that offered the basic materials of the "Han" people's traditional education. But the fact that they were set off, as *the* three, from the dynasties that followed suggests that China had become decisively new as the Chou went down. We have noted that the Confucian legends of sage-kings exemplified the cultural ideals of their transmitters and perpetuators. Not the *san-tai*, a vital part of their subject, but the "Han *tai*," the age of their enshrinement, became the prototype in the long imperial, Confucian-bureaucratic succession. It was during the Han dynasty that recognizable shape was first given to the culture, social structure, political system, and economy of China as they were known until recent times. And more than anything else, it was the political system of Han that gave China its unique stamp.

Some have spoken of the political system of China as oriental despotism, others as benevolent monarchism. It was a system headed by a powerful emperor, the "illustrious theocrat" (as one philologist has translated the word *huang-ti*); a system staffed by a class of literati bureaucrats, an educated elite to whom the tasks of administration were entrusted; and a system moved by an ideology based on the moralistic, worldly ethic of Confucius. Though foreign invaders hostile to Chinese civilization and strange creeds redolent of mysticism and egoism entered China again and again, nothing was able to shake these three pillars of the political structure of China, until the advent of the modern world. Despite its ultimate disappearance, the political system — and from it derived a major part of China's great culture — demonstrated a stability and continuity unrivaled except by Pharaonic Egypt, a stability and continuity that produced, not stagnation in China, but ever new manifestations of social and intellectual life.

How did this system arise and what were the elements that gave it strength? Answers to these questions will tell us much, not only about China, but about the nature of political systems in general.

During the early Han period, two great problems dominated the thoughts of men. One was the problem of how to establish power, and the other the problem of men's relationship to power. The solutions to those problems created the traditional political system of China: monarchy and bureaucracy as the power institutions, Confucian ideology as the regulator of their relationships with men. Other societies and other times have faced these same problems, but few have solved them with such permanence as China of the Han dynasty, though the people of the Han period themselves were hardly aware of the durability of the system they created. The formation of the Han state and the solutions to these problems arose from a situation in which total, unfettered power had been let loose in society, and from the reaction of articulate, sensitive, fearful men to a system that regarded them as tools rather than as human beings.

When Ch'in Shih Huang-ti united the empire for the first time in the history of China, an all-powerful emperor ruled the realm. When the kings of Chou disappeared, the tie with the old legitimate order was broken. The feudal aristocracy was destroyed, and the ancestral lands of this class fell into the hands of peasant landowners. A new system of administration came into existence. Bureaucrats, not aristocrats, became the administrators of the provinces. The old domains were split up into districts and counties, whose boundaries cut through the domains, just like the boundaries of the French *préfectures* after the French Revolution. A reign of law superseded the reign of tradition. In the revolutionary fervor of change, the literary works of the Confucianists that reminded men of the old order were destroyed. Legalism became the official and sole ideology of the Ch'in empire.

But the establishment of the Ch'in empire did not lead to the new order for which the Legalists had hoped. True, great changes had taken place: conflict abated; public order was instituted; there was impressive economic development, furthered by the standardization (abstract, impersonal, hence un-Confucian) of weights and measures, coinage, and the like; the Great Wall was constructed to free China from the threat of foreign (mainly Hsiung-nu, or "Hun") invasion. However, the greater the energy of the Ch'in, the more wealth was needed to carry out these projects and the more ruthless was the marshaling of labor. Impoverishment ensued, and political repression. "Those who use the past to oppose the present must be exterminated," cried Li Ssu. It was the Ch'in that was exterminated, and the Han dynasty was born.

Though there were still men in the court of Han Kao-tsu (Liu Pang or Liu Chi) who held to the doctrines of Legalism, the most articulate voices of the period demanded a return to the more humane doctrines of the past. Lu Chia called for a change in human morality, for an emphasis on altruism. So great was the fear of absolutism that he reverted to the old Taoist idea that nonrule was the best way of ruling. Chia I called for changes in the institutions bequeathed by Ch'in. The people, he stated (echoing Mencius), are the foundation of empire, and the ruler must rule for them, not himself. But perhaps the most important change in the spirit of these men was in their attitude toward reason. Reason, with its connotations of impersonal abstractness (a state repugnant, as we have seen, to Confucius), was regarded as the source of much of the evil that had befallen China, and as an antidote to reason there arose something in the nature of a new religious faith. The cosmological teachings of the Warring States period (especially the *yin-yang* teaching, most prominently elaborated by Tsou Yen, fl. fourth to third centuries B.C.) were now raised to the status of religion. Heaven was no longer simply the cosmos, or the fundamental law of the universe, but became active and morphic. The philosophical beliefs of the early Han were clearly religious. There was great interest in the divinations books of classical times. Geomancy, fortune-telling, interpretation of auguries were much in vogue. And religion became a powerful weapon in the hands of those who sought to curb the absolutism of the imperial institution. Belief in the supreme authority of Heaven came before belief in the supreme authority of the emperor.

The greatest figure in the building of the doctrines of Han Confucianism was Tung Chung-shu, adviser to Emperor Wu. It was he who, building especially on the *Book of*

Documents and "Mencius", established the doctrine of the "mark of the mandate of Heaven." The emperor ("Son of Heaven") ruled by virtue of an investiture from the supreme authority of Heaven. But it was not for the emperor to interpret this mandate as he saw fit, for the mandate was to be exercised for Heaven's purposes, nothing less than the establishment of cosmic harmony, harmony in a continuum of the social and natural worlds. If these purposes were not fulfilled, if social harmony dissolved under an emperor's administration, then "marks," social and natural together, would appear in the empire — natural calamities and human disaster. Disorder, oppression, cruelty, floods, droughts, the "trembling of heaven and earth", and other such cosmic phenomena were signs that the mandate was being withdrawn. At such times the rule of the emperor and the existence of the whole dynasty were in danger. Unless the emperor conformed again to the way of Heaven, all would be lost.

Here, with this doctrinal intervention by Tung Chungshu, we meet again a problem raised in our discussion of Confucius himself. Was Confucius a "democrat," concerned primarily with the rights of the people? It has been suggested that Confucius' governing concept was rather something else, traditionalism. And similarly, although Han Confucianists made permanent the obligation of a dynasty to prove itself with Heaven, as it were — to answer, perhaps with its life, for the swelling of popular distress — this implied a bureaucratic, not a democratic check. For, just insofar as the bureaucracy made good its escape from imperial control of the Ch'in Legalist variety (in which officials were merely manipulated "means," not the "ends" implied in the Confucian affinity for an antibarbarian high culture), the bureaucracy could operate in its private interests, as distinct from the public interests of the state (i.e., the emperor, his position demanding defense of the central power against any drain to private sectors). And in their own private interests, officials might then contribute (and recurrently did so throughout subsequent Chinese history) to an ominous neglect of public (i.e., imperial) functions, a neglect that could bring the peasant masses to despairing violence. Under these circumstances, the moralistic assumptions of Confucianism obviously suited the officials' situation: let the omens — the violence, for one — be interpreted as censure of the imperial virtue, and dynasties might fall but bureaucracies pick up their thread with the next in dynastic line. The "mandate of Heaven" doctrine proved not so much a defense of the people, mitigating absolutism, as a defense of literati in their possession of the state apparatus and their recurrent draining of the public power into their private hands.

Does all this mean that, in rejecting the "democratic" interpretation of "mandate of Heaven" as excessively sentimental, one opts for utter cynicism, with the "mandate" seen as merely a cover for rational calculators of their own economic interest? No, this would be a crude distortion. Tung Chung-shu himself, after all, was no private predator, but one who saw with great clarity the social dangers of usurpation of land by great families (which were more and more, in Han times, families of bureaucratic, not feudal provenance). It would be historically fantastic to conjure up a China dominated by Confucianists whose doctrine was empty (as *they* would know, but not the mass of outsiders), merely a hoax successfully perpetrated by generation after generation of initiates. Rather, Han Confucianism was genuinely persuasive, a doctrine of stability appropriate to the staying power of the bureaucratic Han type of state. The anti-Confucian Ch'in revolution — which, starkly imperial itself, cleared the ground for the Confucian-tempered imperial state from then on — was never quite repeated. Violence came, swept away dynasties, but never (until modern times) swept away "the system," as the Ch'in had done in their time. Socially conservative as they were socially established, Han officials ultimately really assumed a Confucian cast of mind. They were open to a traditionalist philosophy, and to religious convictions about Heaven and its mandate (implying *adjustment* — new dynasties, not new social orders) that corresponded to their social commitments to harmony on earth.

The moral duties of the emperor, then, lay in raising his imperfect subjects to the level of full human beings. "Heaven has created the people and their nature is good," said Tung Chung-shu, "but their character is not yet completely good. Hence Heaven has set up the King to rule them with goodness. This is the intent of Heaven. . . . The King is he who receives the Will of Heaven in order to perfect the nature of the people." This meant that it was the duty of the ruler to make of his people full human beings, to give them awareness of the fullness of human life. But since it was the will of Heaven that gave the ruler this task, it was also the will of Heaven that could withdraw its mandate. The sanctions behind these Confucian injunctions were thus hardly moral or philosophical, but openly religious. It is not coincidental that it was Emperor Wu, Tung Chung-shu's at times unwilling patron, who reestablished the great *feng-shan* imperial sacrifices to Heaven and Earth, sacrifices that were religiously carried out by all succeeding emperors.

Confucianism and Legalism, then, are opposed as intellectual abstractions, as integral creeds. The Ch'in dynasty preserved this opposition in a relatively pure state, "burned the (Confucian) books" and "buried the (Confucian) scholars," and set out to level (Legalistically) the population beneath the throne, to regulate society by impersonal, universal *fa*, or "law." But history is hard on intellectual abstractions and the integrity of creeds; as a unified empire system the Ch'in enjoyed little history, and the Han made adjustments — long-lasting adjustments, persisting beyond the Han — in the harsh, unviable Ch'in system. Confucianism (though not, of course, unaffected by other creeds) became embodied in bureaucracy, as Legalism (with the same *caveat*) had become embodied in monarchy, and these two bodies became locked together in both a bout and an embrace.

The bureaucracy welcomed the monarchical centralization as a condition of its existence, but it resisted the monarch's Legalist propensity, on the Ch'in model, to make his officials mere tools, dead counters to be moved around like any others. A Confucian feeling for hierarchy (though not on a feudal basis) and personal relationships strained against Legalist impersonal leveling. The appropriate Confucian ideal of rule by virtuous example (*te-chih*) was pitted against the imperial ideal of a Legalist rule of law (*fa-chih*). Institutionally, the contest was equal: Han bureaucracy gave in to monarchy and served its power purposes; but Han monarchy gave in to bureaucracy, too, and the Legalists, though coloring Confucianism, disappeared as an in·

tegral school, while Confucianism was "established" by the state. And the Confucianists' intellectual supremacy was the measure of the bureaucracy's check on the monarch's pretensions to a truly ultimate power. It was a therapeutic check for monarchy, preserving it after the Ch'in from the Ch'in *hubris,* and making the Han system, with its vital tension (bureaucracy and monarchy as *counterpoised collaborators*) last long enough (transcending the dynasties of Han name) to bequeath that name to the perennial Chinese people.

Background

Han: II, Confucianists and Landownership

THE PATTERN

One of the long-lasting antifeudal conventions that became established in the Han system was the Ch'in convention of equal inheritance among all sons (promulgated for Han in 127 B.C.). Feudal primogeniture perpetuates inequality, since land is left concentrated in individual hands. For this reason Han emperors, and subsequent dynasts on the Han model, favored constant pressure for the fragmentation of landholdings, to counteract any protofeudal, anticentral private aggrandizement. There was a basis, in Confucianism's own antifeudal, state-centered orientation, for Confucian accord with this imperial policy, and the great Confucianist, Tung Chung-shu, in mid-second century B.C., advocated *hsien-t'ien*, "limitation of fields," an egalitarian policy of checking private accumulation and the consequent social imbalance, which was a threat to social order.

But what had produced the threat? The Han loosening of the Ch'in check rein on officials permitted the latter to use their public powers in their private interest, and their Confucian commitment to state service accorded badly with their Confucian commitment to family prosperity. Landowning, providing the wealth and leisure for study of the Confucian curriculum, was becoming more closely associated with the Confucianized bureaucracy that depended on such study, and officials tended to strengthen their power in the sector from which they had sprung (or to establish their power there in the first place, as a hedge against the insecurity of bureaucratic tenure).

Hence, in Han times, we find a development of the private sector of the economy. There was increasing acquisition of land by officials, who could give it, to a varied extent, the protection of their position. Thus, the bureaucracy, part of the state apparatus, was also a body of landowners anxious to make the most of the perquisites of office, and their immediate private interests conflicted with those of the centralized government of which they were a part. A pattern emerged in Han that recurred in subsequent dynasties: the pattern described in the folk saying (originally a sally by the Legalist Han Fei Tzu), *chung pao*, "middle replete (or satisfied)": not peasants, not emperor, but officials (at worst) denuding the first and defrauding the second.

Land tax, the financial mainstay of the dynasty, became harder to collect as officials preempted more land and withdrew it (as far as they could) from the tax rolls. Reduction in tax collected led to decline in state expenditures for water works, military defenses against despoilers, and so on, and thus to decline in productivity. Unhappily but inevitably for the smallholder, without official connections, this worsening of his prospects coincided with a heightening of the exactions of officials, who were trying to shift the burden of their own financial dues to the vulnerable outsiders. And this increased the need for credit. Into the breach stepped the moneylender (most likely a large, relatively well-protected landholder, from the officials' milieu), his usurious rates greasing the path to expropriation. More land came to those who had enough already not only to let them resist such depredations but to commit them. And so the concentration of land ensued, the growth of ominous private interests, threatening the state that sought ideally to fragmentize private interest, but whose bureaucracy was staffed by the very people who had to be most controlled.

"HSIEN-T'IEN": THE LANDLORD-OFFICIALS
AGAINST THEMSELVES

When *hsien-t'ien*, then, appeared to the government as a social remedy, it was to a government, or governors, riven by conflicting impulses. However cogent the policy might seem to landholders in their official capacity, to landholders in their private capacity "limiting fields" was not congenial. Desiring the preservation of the state and the mitigation of unrest (these conditions reinforcing each other), they devised, as officials, a policy for the state in the abstract — a reasonably logical policy, given the end in view. But in concrete individual circumstances the psychology of the situation, not the logic, prevailed, and the policy fell into abeyance.

Tung Chung-shu, as we have indicated, charged that peasant misery stemmed principally from the usurpation of land by great families, and he advocated limits to the extent of private property. Much time had to pass, but in effect his recommendation was adopted in 6 B.C., when it was decreed that no one had the right to possess more than 30 *ch'ing* (ca. 450 acres) of *ming-t'ien* (i.e., freely alienable private property, as distinct from domain land, the dwindling remnants of feudal fiefs held by connections of the imperial house). As the *History of the Former Han Dynasty* (the second in the great line of Dynastic Histories, after Ssu-ma Ch'ien's prototype, *Shih-chi, Records of the Historian*) indicates, this law was never seriously applied — which brings us back to the psychology of the situation: however much their prosperity depended on the existence of a state apparatus for them to manipulate, landlord-officials would not consistently enforce a law that was abstractly in the state's interest if it was concretely a limitation on their immediate power. It was this situation, not the much vaunted theory of the "mandate of Heaven," which seems to have been the one great *material* restraint always existing against imperial absolutism. Theoretically, there was no restraint; officials should have been mere channels of an untrammeled imperial will. But officials would not cooperate in their own despoliation, which the *public interest* (represented by the emperor, who *was* the state, in theory) might seem to demand. For if possession of public power by officials was desirable to them in large part because of their private aspirations, then strengthening of the public power was not desirable to them if it was at the expense of their private aspirations. This was true for Han, at the beginning of Chinese imperial-bureaucratic history, and it was true for Ch'ing, at the end of it.

THE WANG MANG INTERREGNUM (9–23 A.D.)

This was the social situation that helped to bring a "strong man" to power (signaling the end of the "Former Han" dynasty), and that helped to sap the power he attained. Wang Mang was a member of an influential clan related by marriage to the Han imperial house. After becoming the most prominent man in the state, and ultimately regent for a child emperor, he deposed the latter in 9 A.D. and proclaimed himself emperor in a new dynasty, the "Hsin."

He never had a dynastic successor. He died in 23 A.D., defeated, and remained forever after loathed by Confucianists, a traditional bogey man. His centralizing policies heightened the tension between monarch and Confucianists to the point of conflict of interests, and Wang, more than most vigorous monarchs, proved vulnerable to the censures of historians. For he had the bad luck to be sandwiched between two dynasties called Han; with the Liu family restored in the "Later Han" period (25–220 A.D.), Wang Mang became fixed in the histories as not just an unsuccessful dynast, but as that dreadfully un-Confucian disloyal thing — a usurper. In Pan Ku's *History of the Former Han Dynasty* (late first century A.D.), the first successor to Ssu-ma Ch'ien's great work in the series of Dynastic Histories, Wang Mang's reign was described, not in the "Basic Annals" section, but in a *chuan* or biography. And this was located in a disgrace place, directly after the discussion of "Barbarous Tribes."

Some modern commentators have made Wang out as an idealistic crackpot. He did indeed make tactical errors. He was certainly overoptimistic about simple fiat in a society in which orders had to be carried out by men with a possible interest in subverting them. Yet, he seems to have been rationally aware of just what social areas and problems had to be dealt with if society were not to collapse. It was in dealing with these that he met his major opposition, as he took policies in harmony with the outer, public strain in Confucianism and tried to push them, "Legalisticially," through Confucianists' private defenses.

In the year 9 A.D., Wang made a more radical attempt at *hsien-t'ien* than any the Han had broached. He decreed that private property should be limited to 100 *mou* (ca. 42 acres) per owner. He tried to forbid the purchase and sale of land (i.e., to impugn the very conception of private property); as a corollary he forbade mortgage loans, since these could become, in effect, the means of selling land. And he had in mind, or just as a gleam in his eye, the revival of the *ching-t'ien* (well-field) system, Mencius' egalitarian ideal.

Wang tried hard. He made great enemies. He made no friends because he accomplished nothing, and at the end of three years he had to rescind his edict and allow the resumption of free commerce in land.

Another of Wang's policies had also had a Han precedent but no honest Han enforcement. This was the idea of treasuries and granaries that should be kept "ever normal." The *History of the Former Han Dynasty* attributes this conception to a minister of one of the pre-Ch'in "Warring States." The minister noted that if grain was too expensive it hurt the consumers, and if grain was too cheap it hurt the growers. Merchants and rich families, he said, took advantage of price fluctuations and hoarded grain. And so the government should purchase when the price was low, and sell to the market when the price was high.

Wang Mang pushed this policy, and in a companion move he put the state in the money-lending business, with loans at a rate much more moderate than the going private rates. Just as the "Five Equalizations Policy" (the granary scheme) was directed against the use of wealth for exploitative, speculative hoarding, so this loan policy was directed against the use of wealth for private usury. Both these programs, naturally enough, were disliked by the wealthy; and there was little or no visible help to the poor. Officials who managed the state granary plan, for instance, diverted much of the proceeds into manipulations of their own. Then Wang further alienated a large part of the population by new taxes. These were not given time to produce the benefits they were supposed to disseminate. Provocative to the public, yet they brought in too little to the state. This led to debasement of the currency, and the regime went further down hill. When border troubles and natural disaster came — Central Asian tribal revolts and a deadly shift in the course of the Yellow River — Wang could not survive. The story is that in his last months, in 23 A.D., he sat up with almost no sleep or food, incessantly sending down edicts while nobody listened — a doomed Macbeth, deserted, the avengers coming on all sides.

HAN RESTORATION

The beginning of the end for Wang Mang was the peasant rising of the "Red Eyebrows," who were turbulent in the northeast, in the area of present-day Shantung, by the year 18 A.D. This uprising was not directed against Wang Mang in his character as usurper, nor even exclusively against Wang's regime on the grounds of its own demerits. Rather, it represented a tide of peasant revulsion against the whole ruling order, a tide that Wang had tried and failed to dam up. The landed interests hated Wang for his attempts to curb their power. When Wang was frustrated, partly by their hatred, and failed to curb their power, his regime became to peasants the last excruciating straw of social oppression. And so Wang's "dynasty" was disowned both by gentry-official Han legitimists and rebellious peasant Red Eyebrows. Each of these groupings seems to have seen him as something like a class enemy in the service of the other.

The two extremes, then, were not united by their opposition to Wang Mang. The Red Eyebrows did not fight for the Han, but themselves had to be dispatched before the Han could be firmly restored. The Later Han dynasty was fairly begun with Emperor Kuang-wu, who came to power in 25 A.D. (after two years in the shadow of another Han claimant). He had cleared the field by 36 A.D. The dread Malthusian correctives, misery and massacre, had taken off some of the social pressure, and a period of peace began, with a semblance of dynastic health. There was some redistribution of vacated land, but it never went beyond the merest tinkering with the social order. The forces of rebellion were exhausted. Yet, however much time it might take, nothing could keep the cancer of social unrest from growing again to mortal size. In 184 A.D., the Taoist rebellion of the "Yellow Turbans" erupted, portending centuries of social turmoil and Confucian eclipse.

Reading

Swann, Nancy Lee, *Food and Money in Ancient China* (Princeton: Princeton University Press, 1950).

Dubs, Homer H., *The History of the Former Han Dynasty by Pan Ku* (Baltimore: Waverly Press, 1955), Vol. III.

Bielenstein, Hans, *The Restoration of the Han Dynasty*, Vols. I and II (Stockholm: Bulletin of the Museum of Far Eastern Antiquities, 1954, 1959).

Implications

Bureaucracy, Monarchy, and Social Tensions: Obstacles to a Capitalist Resolution

We suggested (in Chapter 7) that bureaucratic-imperial China (the China established by Ch'in and Han) was both postfeudal and noncapitalist. Feudalism, stage as well as system, was a stage not to a capitalism-in-being, but to a capitalism aborted. "Capitalism" is relevant enough to Han to let us discern "feudalism" in Chou antiquity. But it was a capitalism not strong enough to prevail — only strong enough to elicit forces to smother its potential.

This was the agrarian-bureaucratic state, where land and office were intimately connected, and where landlessness, or the threat of it, recurrently led to rebellion and sometimes to political breakdown. Officials used the state to further private interests on the land, until the state was so weakened that the private interests were threatened. But the bearers of the threat, Chinese peasants, or invaders encouraged by the parlous state of China, were harbingers of revival (though it was sometimes long deferred). The kill was the cure — private interests, protofeudal interests, were so shaken that the state was at last strengthened. The magic combination was always the possession of land plus possession of state (i.e., bureaucratic) influence. When possession of land was so strengthened that there was little or no state left to possess, then some corrective plundering in the private sector restored a state, and restored the possibility of a workable combination. Landed literati-officials made up the combination. Peasants struck it, but they never conclusively shattered it. They might be recruited into this ruling stratum; they never, once and for all, established their own, novel hegemony.

In feudal Europe, too, the landed powers faced peasant jacqueries and never succumbed to them. But the landed, feudal element did eventually succumb to something else, and individuals either went down or joined, in some degree, the enemy: the class, the "bourgeoisie," that struggled not for the proceeds of rent, as peasants and landlords did, but for the proceeds of exchange, trade, and manufacture.

Did anything like this class exist in traditional China? It did. Why, then, when it was time for someone to take up the struggle for antifeudal centralization, did merchants not lead the struggle and make it meaningful, rather than leave it to peasants, who made it comparatively meaningless? Why did a bourgeoisie in China that began weak stay weak, qualitatively, and leave the society that gave it birth unchallenged — while a bourgeoisie in Europe that began weak became strong, and changed its social matrix out of all recognition?

Landed bureaucracy as lure

Trade had its attractions in China from a very early time. The rise from poor to wealthy merchant was not uncommon. Perhaps it occurred more frequently, proportionately, than the rise from peasant to gentry status by orthodox means — that is, frugal land accumulation, education of a son, his success in the Confucian examinations. But because, by and large, land was already alienable when the Han put their stamp on China, and because money talked, a merchant could hope to acquire landlord status for his family and the chance to put together the land, learning, and office combination. Han set the style of a freer social mobility than feudal Europe authorized, and there were solid inducements in China to seize on the chances to move.

For one thing (and here Europe was hardly different), more prestige accrued to landed families than to merchant families. "Treacherous merchant" was a familiar tag for traders and middlemen. The Confucianist-Legalist debate (first century B.C.) on "salt and iron" records a literati protest against the fostering of commerce. The important point is this: the system gave low prestige to the merchant but, unlike the feudal European system, provided the channel (though sometimes clogged) through which he could acquire high prestige. He need not feel he must wreck the system and create his own, in which he could arrogate high prestige to himself.

For another thing, there were material inducements. For land became (and remained until modern times) the best gilt-edged investment. Especially when the population showed a tendency to rise, there was strong competition for land, hence a rise in the rates of rent. When so many needed land for subsistence, the best profits came from extortion; normally, men would seek title to land to fragmentize it for its yields in rent, rather than to consolidate it for production for the market. And land was a safer stake than any market commodities. For these were destructible, while land was not, even in periods of anarchy. It was a social paradox: the land system that recurrently led to the threat of anarchy (through tax pressure leading to alienation of the land of those not officially well-connected) appealed because of the threat of anarchy itself.

Of course, as land rents rose, land prices rose. As it became more difficult for a peasant to buy land, it became more necessary for him to be a tenant, and the rents rose again. This, together with the minute size of the rental fragment, made it unlikely that the peasant would acquire a surplus, which he would need for acquiring the larger area he needed. Into this vicious circle stepped the money lenders — none other than the landlords, skimming the cream twice.

Thus, moral prestige and a material sure thing made up the lure of the landowning, noncommercial status.

LANDED BUREAUCRACY AS THREAT

When carrot comes, can stick be far behind? Merchants felt not only the pull but the push of the bureaucratic system. Their mercantile status was legally weak. There was no real provision for property rights, contractual relationships, or corporate activity. Law, largely penal, not civil, was a prop for the state not the individual. The state set up monopolies (e.g., in salt and iron), at the expense of private traders — or rather, restricted trade in protected commodities to a closed circle of private traders, bound to the state for the privilege. And merchants were acutely vulnerable to bureaucratic "squeeze." Hence, merchants had to try to contrive a relationship of interdependence with officials. Unable to find protection in law, merchants sought to establish personal connections of good will with individual bureaucrats, through gifts and services. Golden eggs had to be doled out to save merchants' necks, to stave off the always possible capricious expropriation.

Sometimes it did not work. In the absence of legal security, and when personal arrangements failed, officials might show their social power in drastic, sudden ways. Here is Ssu-ma Ch'ien's *Shih-chi* (tr. Burton Watson) on an episode in the reign of Han Wu-ti:

. . . charges were brought forward all over the empire against men who attempted to conceal their wealth from the levy; practically every family of middling means or over found itself under accusation. . . . The emperor dispatched parties of assistants under the imperial secretary and the commandant of justice to . . . examine the charges of concealed wealth. The wealth confiscated from the people was . . . cash . . . slaves . . . fields . . . houses. Practically all the merchants of middling or better means were ruined. The district officials found themselves with more and more funds at their disposal, due to the salt and iron monopolies and the confiscations of wealth.

The *Shih-chi* was a model for subsequent dynastic histories. This story was something of a model, too.

Yet, on the whole, there came to be a *modus vivendi*. Merchants existed, even flourished, but precariously, in a world of official supremacy and hence of unofficial understandings. It was a world in which the economic spirit reflected the general Confucian spirit, one of "art of life," where personal, tacit accommodations took the place of mechanical operations. Not only the existence of squeeze but the acceptance of squeeze, as something to be expected, shows how weak the capitalist spirit was. The western censorious attitude on squeeze derives from the fact that, in Europe, "moral uprightness" in money matters had a historical connection with quantitative book-keeping. And this was a regular feature of an ideally impersonal system. It had no counterpart in China, where the nearest thing to economic rule was a possibly "regular" irregularity, a product of personal arrangements.

OFFICE AS A COMMODITY

The "squeeze" situation, the peculiar relation between bureaucracy and business, made up part of the story of corruption, which was one of the causes of dynastic decline. And when dynasties were in decline, bureaucracy *became* business, to some extent — office became a field of business investment. That is, the declining dynasty, being financially distressed, resorted to sale of office. This had no Confucian sanction, of course. But Confucian opposition to sale of office was just as unrealistic as the opposition to undue land accumulation, the latter expressed in the *hsien-t'ien* movement for limitation of holdings. *Hsien-t'ien* was advocated by precisely the same Tung Chung-shu who abhorred sale of office and fostered the testing of Confucian learning as the only proper road to office.

For the fact was that the state needed compensation for the strength it lost through bureaucracy's private aggrandizement. And office *could* be sold. But it was an illusion to think it might save the state, for it was socially destructive;

crass investors in office could only compound the injustices that were stirring up rebellion. *Hsien-t'ien* theoretically might save the state, but socially it could not be implemented. So the ostensible cure for the state that could really, socially, be applied was a poison — it would not work as a cure. And the cure that theoretically might work could not really, socially, be applied. In either case, Confucianism seemed tarnished by its official defenders (defender officials).

In this situation, we may expect finally one of two alternatives. There may be an initially anti-Confucian revolt from the lower reaches of society, as we find at the end of the Later Han, with the "Yellow Turbans." To them, Confucianism seemed more of a class tool and symbol than a universal, applicable idea. Or we may see the temporary emergence of a "strong man" from within the ranks of the official class itself. This is the man who claims to make Confucianism once again significant, not just symbolic, by enforcing antiprivate measures on a reluctant, though ostensibly public officialdom. And this we found at the end of the Former Han, with Wang Mang. But neither Former Han nor Later Han, nor T'ang, nor Sung, nor Ming offered a viable capitalist alternative at critical junctures like these. For that, we must wait for modern China, the age of the treaty ports.

Background

Han: III, Syncretism and Contact with "Barbarians"

SYNCRETISM

Among the "Hundred Schools" we have noted especially the big three, Confucianism, Taoism, and Legalism. To present them as neatly separated is too schematic, a tidy bibliographer's fiction. In Han times, certainly, syncretism was the rule; these three commingled among themselves, and each one absorbed a great deal from other strains of thought. Yet, Confucianism was primary as the central absorptive body. "Yin-yang" and "Five Elements" (otherwise known as the "five powers") were prominent parts of the Han Confucian amalgam.

As a pair, *yin* and *yang*, separately named but inseparable, suggested a sort of syncretism. Opposites interpenetrated: female and male, dark and light, and so on. Appropriately, then, as a school, *yin-yang* was available when syncretists collected schools of thought, blurring their lines (a good *yin-yang* conception) in a composite. And "five elements" theory, too, which was linked early with *yin-yang* (see Chapter 7), had its own natural affinity with the syncretizing purpose. The five elements, succeeded one another in ascendancy; they suggested an order of nature. But history, too, was brought into the system, with the "Five Emperors" (from Fu Hsi on) appearing in series, each with an element in the ascendant, and a color, and a direction (center, east, south, west, north). Tung Chung-shu, the most important thinker in adapting Confucianism for a state orthodoxy, was a *yin-yang*, five-elements theorist *par excellence*; the state was a microcosm of the universe, and the emperor should govern in accordance with nature (mercy more than punishment, as Heaven favors *yang* over *yin*, with only a touch of *yin* necessary to bring autumn to winter, punishment to death, things to emptiness). The Han spirit of homogenization could hardly have been better served, or symbolized. It is small wonder that the five elements dominated the city plan of Loyang (in eastern Honan), the capital city of the Later Han. Gates and palaces represented the "Red Bird of the South" and the other mythological animals and colors in the five-elements world. For the capital city (and the Han tombs, laid out in the five directions) stood for the basic Han cosmogony.

This syncretic philosophy was important in setting the tone of Han art, especially the art of bronze mirrors. Cloud chariots, winged horses, dragons, and birds brought intimations of immortality and other worlds. And they blended with symbolic representations of *yin-yang* and the five elements, which were meant to be kept in balance, to keep the world and the cosmos in equilibrium.

Ssu-ma Ch'ien, too, in his great history, the *Shih-chi*, worked with the general Han assumptions of cycle and sympathy: an order of dynastic successions and an association of qualities in the individual dynasties. Each dynasty had to come and had to go; and each dynasty had a characteristic virtue and a corresponding flaw. Yet, for all this profoundly deterministic spirit (the same spirit of melancholy that accepted the "times," the mysterious "times," as the factor that kept Confucius just a "throneless king"), the historian wrote as a moralist. Men were judged, lessons implied, pointers to action — meaningful action — given. Determinism and voluntarism were locked together in Ssu-ma Ch'ien's work, quite like *yin* and *yang*, and in the Han Confucian amalgam. An inner intellectual tension mirrored the tension in Han political society; and both were tense with life, the essence of persistence and stability.

The Han search for wholeness meant the weaving of "warp" and "woof." The *ching*, the Classics, were warp, the repositories of standards for achieving social order. The *wei-shu* or apocryphal books were woof, the speculative material that linked the ethical realm of history with cosmology. Tung Chung-shu's *Ch'un-ch'iu fan-lu* (*General Principles of the "Spring and Autumn"*) may be considered a *wei-shu* specimen, with its blending of naturalism and ethics, its references to omens and portents as guides for human action in balancing the universe.

In literature, the poignancy of Confucius and Ssu-ma Ch'ien permeated the *sao* poem, the basic form of the *Ch'u Tz'u* or *Songs of Ch'u* (nearer to *Singspiel*, perhaps, than song). Ch'ü Yüan, the poet of the *Li Sao*, the earliest poem (pre-Han) in this Han collection, became the prototype of the loyal minister whose integrity costs him his place at court. Though he rises to a higher plane than this evil earthly world, invokes the spirits and roams the universe, he never really escapes the earth, the despair that accompanies him, the death that awaits him and that he finally seeks. There is something Confucian in the ethic here, something Taoist in the feeling — and something barbarian in the origins. For the ancient state of Ch'u, in the central valley of the Yangtze, was originally (though not by "Warring States" times) culturally outside the pale of China. In the ultimate acceptance of its literature as Han (the Han *fu*, or prose poem, derived from the *sao* style) and one of its families as the House of Han (the founders of this quintessentially Chinese dynasty were a family from an area ruled by Ch'u in the third century B.C.), we see one side of the Confucian approach to "barbarians": assimilation.

BARBARIANS

In 214 B.C., only seven years after his unification of the empire, Ch'in Shih Huang-ti pushed his dominions south into the areas of modern Kwangtung, Kwangsi, and northern Vietnam. The south, being suitable for agriculture, was a more penetrable region than the arid area north of the Great Wall for the established sedentary Chinese way of life. A Chinese minority settled in the south, became partly barbarized at first, and then, with new recruits from north China, began to more than hold its own.

Emperor Kao-tsu (Liu Pang), the Han founder, consolidated Chinese influence after the chaotic years of transition between Ch'in and Han. For example, an independent kingdom had appeared around modern Canton, with Chinese leadership over the relatively primitive Yüeh tribesmen. In 196 B.C. the king was induced to accept Han suzerainty, and more annexations followed. The Han continued to send Chinese into the new regions, and to make Chinese (to a large extent) out of the natives of those areas. Local officials and private scholars established Confucian schools.

In the north and west, the Chinese faced virile, nomadic peoples who were relatively impervious to the benign assimilative influence of Confucian schools. Here, in the main, was where Han military history was made (and a good part of Han economic history, too, as a consequence). The Chinese had been fighting in the north ever since the Spring and Autumn Period. The people whom they called the Hsiung-nu were forced to unite by the Ch'in completion of the Great Wall and control of the Ordos region (in the bend of the Yellow River). Han Kao-tsu was almost captured in 200 B.C., when the Hsiung-nu won a great victory and reduced the Han to a peace policy. A Chinese princess was given to the nomads' ruler, the *Shan-yü*, and the Han were committed to send annual "gifts." Not until 133 B.C., in the reign of the great Wu-ti, who strengthened the Chinese central power, did the Han cease to pay for protection and turn back to self-assertion. It brought the Chinese forcefully into Korea and Central Asia.

In Korea, a state called Wei-shih Ch'ao-hsien had been established by Chinese, but it was outside the jurisdiction of Han. In 109–108 B.C., Wu-ti destroyed the state, to deny it to the northern Hsiung-nu, who had expanded from Mongolia to Manchuria, and he went on to incorporate Korea, organized into four commanderies, in the Han empire. Direct Chinese control over Korea, especially in the northwest and center, lasted for about 400 years. The so-called Lo-lang culture, with its center near present-day Pyongyang in north

Korea, remains for archaeologists one of the greatest repositories of splendid Han remains.

The main thrust against the Hsiung-nu was in the west.
In 139 B.C., the envoy Chang Ch'ien set out on his famous
odyssey that took him deep into western Asia. His mission
(a failure) was to contract an alliance with the Indo-Scyth-
ian Yueh-chih people, whom the Hsiung-nu had harried
from northeast Asia to the area northwest of India, where
they had established the Kushan kingdom. Twice captured
by the Hsiung-nu, Chang Ch'ien nevertheless returned to
Ch'ang-an in 126 B.C., and lived to set out again, in 115 B.C.,
to establish Han relations with Ferghana and Sogdiana. Ferghana fell to the Han in 101 B.C., and the lasting Chinese
interest in the oases of Central Asia (often physically
thwarted, but ever re-indulged) was for the first time firmly
realized. The "Silk Road" for trade with the Roman Empire ran from Ch'ang-an (Sian, in present-day Shensi),
through Tun-huang in Kansu, across the Tarim River basin
and out to the west.

The Hsiung-nu revived during the civil wars at the end of
Wang Mang's rule. Ultimately, under the Later Han, the
Hsiung-nu were split, and they lived along the frontiers as a
tributary people, to rise again in the fourth century A.D. as
part of the wave of barbarian violence that ended the Chinese sway (until Sui, in 589 A.D.) over northern China.

What did the Hsiung-nu experience suggest to the
Chinese about the barbarian nature? Back in the early Han
days of the peace policy, Chia I (201–169 B.C.) recommended
"five baits" to corrupt the nomads with the luxuries of Han.
Their austere, vigorous way of life was seen as the source of
the Hsiung-nu military menace. The Hsiung-nu were
hooked with the poisoned fruit, and the Han were able to
match their military effectiveness. But they had to match it
recurrently, because the very Chinse products that soothed
the savage beast also whetted the savage (not yet *quite*
soothed) appetite. The Han pattern of relations with the
Hsiung-nu became part of the Han model for subsequent
Confucian-imperial Chinese history: China's foreign relations consisted of tribute system ("exchange of presents")
and war. When Tung Chung-shu memorialized that the
Hsiung-nu were not susceptible to *li* ("propriety"), only to *li*

("profits"), he laid down the line for Ch'ing dynasty memorialists, almost two millenia later, as they saw the western tea-for-opium traders chase their profits and confirm their barbarian identities.

Reading

Tjan Tjoe Som, *Po Hu T'ung, The Comprehensive Discussion in the White Tiger Hall: A Contribution to the History of Classical Studies in the Han Period*, Vol. I (Leiden: E. J. Brill, 1949).

Lattimore, Owen, *Inner Asian Frontiers of China* (Boston: Beacon Press, 1962). Paperback (original edition 1940).

Yü Ying-shih, *Trade and Expansion in Han China: A Study in the Structure of Sino-Barbarian Economic Relations* (Berkeley and Los Angeles: University of California Press, 1967).

Implications

Intellectual Implications of Social Stability: (a) Confucianism and Taoism as Philosophical Correlatives

We have suggested (a), that Confucianism was above all a philosophy of stability, the antithesis of change; (b), that it was, accordingly, peculiarly appropriate to Chinese society after the Ch'in revolution, because that society, in its resolution of the tensions of feudalism, was on its way to becoming, to a marked degree, a stable society; (c), that this social stability must not be confused with social peace — that, on the contrary, it encompasses the fact of recurrent internal disorder. A stability that subsumes disorder is a social paradox. Is there any intellectual paradox that parallels this social situation and corroborates the fact of its existence?

Social stability implies an accommodation of different social strata to each other — an accommodation which, though it may be ruptured, is then at least roughly reconstituted, so that the society's quality is not crucially altered. In post-Ch'in bureaucratic society there are, in intellectual terms, precisely this accommodation of differences and these impermanent ruptures of the accommodation. Confucianism and Taoism *belong together* (the part of the subject more prominently treated in this "problem"); and Confucianism and Taoism *oppose each other* (see Chapter 11, below). They belong together and oppose each other intellectually in a socially significant way.

Inasmuch as recurrence is a part of this pattern of accommodation and rupture, description of the pattern for the Han age will involve us in references to a considerably longer span of time than that.

"NATURE" AND "SOCIETY" IN WESTERN AND CONFUCIAN HUMANISM

There is an old saw in China which says that men tend to be Confucianists in office, Taoists when out of office. This should not be taken literally, as though biographies could be written on that basis. But it does say something meaningful; in capsule form it sums up two complicated circumstances. First, it suggests that Confucianism is linked with power and prestige in social life and that Taoism is its converse, implying release from society and social concerns. But, second, it also implies that Confucianism and Taoism, though opposites, somehow belong together, making the whole man, and not so much warring for prominence in Chinese culture as depending on each other to create a culture in which both take part.

What is the opposition between them? It appears in their emphases, respectively, on two concepts that have been opposites by definition, in both much of Chinese and much of western thought: *society* (the Confucian emphasis) and *nature* (the Taoist emphasis). But in China, although society and nature are set apart by definition, they are not polardistant as points of departure for schools of Chinese thinking. Confucianism and Taoism must never be seen as the "classic" and "romantic" of China.

To clarify this statement, to see precisely what the Chinese higher intellectual approach was *not*, we may note some examples from western civilization. In classical Greece, with Socrates, there was an explicit turning from a philosophical interest in the cosmos (the Ionian, "pre-Socratic" philosophy) to a philosophy of man and society. Socrates says to Phaedrus in the Platonic dialogue: "I am a lover of knowledge; and the men who dwell in the city are my teachers, and not the trees or the country." Much later, in the eighteenth century, Samuel Johnson echoed this (and Dr. Johnson was a paladin of classicists, with many of whose attitudes on life and nature the romantics explicitly conflicted). On a journey through France, while others were admiring the scenery, Dr. Johnson testily retorted: "A blade of grass is always a blade of grass, whether in one country or another. . . . Men and women are my subjects of inquiry; let us see how these differ from those we have left behind."

Now, this attitude in classical western humanism had implications for the fine arts — and here we see the germ of distinction between western and Confucian humanism: in the West, as a corollary to the classical emphasis on man and moral cultivation (with which cf. Confucius), there was an absence or depreciation of *landscape* in art. This was true in Greek and Roman art, and in the later classical art deriving from Michelangelo and Raphael; landscape was of merely complementary interest. We have not only the evidence of paintings themselves, but many texts on aesthetics, going into the eighteenth century, which tell us that art is ideally directed toward reflection on human actions and potentialities. We will look in vain, in China, for this rejection of landscape by humanists (though in Han times, to be sure, painting was thought to derive moral value from moral subject-matter). In China, perhaps even more than in Europe, a taste for fine arts became an attribute of the intellectual, the conscious bearer of the traditions of civilization, and art in China was thoroughly impregnated with feeling for nature. As Confucian civility took stronger hold (a process beginning, for all practical purposes, in Han times and culminating in the Sung era), nature became *the* great subject in the painting treasures of Confucian culture. Portraiture exists, and a good deal of genre painting, but by and

large the theme of Chinese art has been not man but nature — or, at most, man *in* nature. In the high culture of
China something kept Confucianism and Taoism, "society"
and "nature," from flying apart, from showing the "classic-
romantic" fissure on the European model.

TAOIST AND CONFUCIAN "HARMONY"

The important point is this: Nature in Chinese art (the
art of *Confucian* cognoscenti) is not something to which
man is "classically" indifferent (in a western sense), nor something by which man is "romantically" awed, terrified, or ex-
alted (in a western sense), but something in which man is
Taoistically absorbed. Man is not separated from nature either by intellectual discrimination or by emotional response; he is one with nature, and lives with it in harmony.
Chinese landscape suggests, for the most part, that man fits
as naturally into his surroundings as the trees and mountains do. Nature is not merely observed, for observation implies separation of ego and object — a separation which, for
the Taoists, isolates the self, thus condemning it to the striving they hold vain and to the suffering they see as the inevitable concomitant. It is identification with nature that ban-
ishes consciousness, a consciousness that in the last analysis
is always and ominously of self. That is why Chinese aesthetics, with their important Taoist component, prompt the
viewer to lose himself in the picture. One of the most famous conventions is that of the pygmy figures winding their
way into infinite gorges or wreaths of cloud: they truly belong *in* nature, not on the outside looking in. And living
men belong in the painting just as much as the painted men
belong in nature. The famous Sung painter Kuo Hsi, in his
Essay on Landscape, suggested that the spectator should seem
to stumble into the landscape — a painting should have a
"foreground so near it might block one's path." And this
is the concern, too, that injects the principle of "psychological symmetry" into so much of Chinese landscape.
Objective symmetry is not desired, for in its very completeness it keeps the observer out. But asymmetry leads man
into the natural scene depicted, for *his mind* completes the
formal design.

Such is the Taoist idea of harmony with the cosmos, and its expression in an art that the Confucian scholar prizes, even though his Confucianism ties him to the world of affairs and action, far from the Taoist natural solitude. We will dwell later on the distinction between Taoist intuition and Confucian didacticism, Taoist anarchism and Confucian political emphasis. But here we must notice that the common concept of *harmony* transcends these distinctions and makes these systems not, to be sure, identical, but correlative.

Formally, in Confucian writings (especially in the Classic, *The Doctrine of the Mean, Chung yung*), and generally in Chinese life and letters, the value of harmony came to be stressed. Harmony was seen as the great norm of both the natural and social worlds; Confucianism and Taoism were equally philosophies of balance, whether man's counterpoise was society or the natural cosmos. Imbalance would have meant man against man, man against nature, in either case a separation between the self and the "other." But Confucianism and Taoism, each in its way, meant union, oneness, the concord and stasis of the eternal pattern.

"NATURE" AND THE "NOBLE SAVAGE"

The aesthetic implications, then, of the Taoist emphasis on nature, as expressed in landscape-painting and poetic reverie, were readily acceptable to civilization-oriented Confucianism. This indicates that the distinction between society and nature as intellectual points of departure does not have to imply a marked intellectual cleavage, whatever the European classic-romantic dichotomy might suggest. There is yet another negative confirmation of Taoism's compatibility with Confucianism, the fact that the Taoist philosophy of nature never had the philobarbarian (hence, obviously and hopelessly non-Confucian) implications of the nature philosophy of the European romantics. Taoism, for all its philosophical bias against civilization in the abstract, never diluted the basic Chinese — and Confucian — hostility to the less highly civilized, often nomadic peoples who impinged on China in the course of history. The nomadic type of life requires a particular combination of pastoral and military virtues; it became more and more anathema to Chinese in the late Chou time and later, as Chinese culture became unequivocally sedentary-agricultural in cast (cf. the origin legends) and the Confucian-pacifist "civilian" strain deepened.

The Chinese antibarbarian style is a familiar one in world history. In the abstract, civilizations have despised these peoples. A Sumerian hymn of the second millenium B.C. reviles the Amorite "who knows no submission . . . who has no house in his life time." In an Egyptian document there is "the miserable stranger . . . his feet are always wandering . . . he battles. . . ." The Babylonian "Wall of the West" was a "civilized contrivance to bar such barbarians, and so were the Egyptian "Wall of the Ruler" and — most famous of all — the Great Wall of China, which the Ch'in finished in the third century B.C. The name *Hsiung-nu* which the Chinese applied to foes north of the Wall had no specific ethnic significance. It denoted the northern nomads in general and referred to their way of life. The character for the *nu* element, while variously written, was usually one that had taken on the meaning of "slave." Recalling Aristotle's dictum that barbarians were "natural slaves," this supremely expresses the Confucian contempt for barbarians — Confucianism being, right to the core, a cult of civilization.

Did Taoism really cross Confucianism in this matter? Let us examine a T'ang poem, "Civilization" (tr. Waley):

To the south-east — three thousand leagues —
The Yuan and Hsiang form into a mighty lake.
Above the lake are deep mountain valleys,
And men dwelling whose hearts are without guile.
Gay like children, they swarm to the tops of the trees;
And run to the water to catch bream and trout.
Their pleasures are the same as those of beasts and birds;
They put no restraint either on body or mind.
Far I have wandered through the Nine Lands;
Wherever I went such manners had disappeared.
I find myself standing and wondering, perplexed,
Whether Saints and Sages have really done us good.

Nothing could be more explicitly Taoist and more explicitly non-Confucian.

Yet, it should be clear that this is the Taoism of a Confucianist; it expresses a sophisticated, introspective attitude characteristic of a civilized self-consciousness. This anti-intellectualism is an intellectual maneuver, this philobarbarism is a civilized attitude. Barbarism here is simply a definition of civilization by antithesis. The pleasure of a flight from civilization is open only to civilized man.

And it is only as this kind of civilized pleasure that barbarism was ever honored in Chinese thought. The Taoist strain introduced this motif of abstract anticivilization, but Taoism never mitigated the contempt of Confucian civilization for concrete, manifest barbarism. Traditional Chinese thought, that is, Taoist or otherwise, did not include approval or admiration of actual historical peoples (not sophisticated concepts) with whom the Chinese clashed in genuine living history.

Once again, as in our discussion of aesthetics, we find that the European dichotomy between classical humanism and romantic bias toward nature is misleading if taken as model for the Confucianism-Taoism relationship. In Europe, the classicists' disparagement of primitive tribal conquerors was countered by the romantic rehabilitation of their reputation. The adjective "Gothic" (from one of the divisions of tribal peoples that conquered the Roman Empire), meaning "rude" in the classical context,. was purged by romantics of its invidious connotation. In *The Decline and Fall of the Roman Empire*, the classicist Edward Gibbon saw the German tribes (and Christianity) as the sappers of civilization; but Mme. de Stael's romantic *On Germany* saw the same tribes as rejuvenators, bringing life back to an effete and worn-out world.

In China, however, Taoism, for all its reverence for nature and the natural, never contributed to historical revisionism: the reputation of real, historical tribal enemies whom the Chinese considered primitive and uncivilized was never rehabilitated by an application of Taoist principles. If philosophical Taoism had implied such softness toward barbarians, it would indeed have been irreconcilable with Confucianism. But Taoism and Confucianism were not irreconcilable; they were only philosophically distinguished from each other by their emphases respectively on nature and society. If they were rivals, their rivalry was ultimately appeasable — an intellectual situation appropriate to a system of social stability.

Indeed, the quietistic formula, *nei sheng wai wang* (inside, sage; outside, king), which we have identified as the cry of Confucian morality against a Legalistic activist autocracy, actually goes back to the Taoist *Chuang Tzu* text. Significantly, the Confucian capacity for syncretism, itself a tribute to harmony, is exercised here in a formula for bringing harmony into being, as social equilibrium, an unforced balance on earth.

CONCLUSION: PHILOSOPHICAL CORRELATION AS REFLECTION OF SOCIETY

Conflict between Confucianism and Taoism was abortive, (a) because they had a common theme, *harmony*, and (b) because that common theme, *harmony*, implied a philosophical deprecation of conflict. (a) and (b) together, the commonness of their theme and the meaning of their theme, damped down any battle between them. Because the clash between Confucianism and Taoism was to a significant extent illusory, their clash in history was relatively unproductive of new conclusions. Intellectual syncretism of Confucianism and Taoism made up a prominent part of Han intellectual history, and syncretism is very much a search for intellectual peace — an attempt to halt the process of change which the clash of opposites often sets in train.

This is at the heart of the problem of the relatively slow pace of intellectual history in traditional, post-Ch'in China; for it is a fact that, as one of the qualities of the socially stable bureaucratic society, Chinese history seems less intellectually crowded than European history, with a milder proliferation of ideas. Confucianism as *traditionalism*, which dominated intellectual life (though there were significant interregna in Confucian rule, which we shall examine), obviously explains, from the standpoint of logical consequence, the slow pace of intellectual change that paralleled the slow pace of social change. But one of the reasons why traditionalism remained *traditional* (i.e., why Confucianism,

from the standpoint of historical or chrono-logical consequence, remained dominant, always recovering from dips in
prestige and acceptance) is that Taoism, its great original
intellectual rival, could be taken into camp to live with Confucianism under the same tent.

SYMBOLIC OPPOSITION AS REFLECTIONS
OF SOCIETY: INTRODUCTION

Thus, the philosophical correlation between Confucianism and Taoism, their fitting together in the high culture of
China, may be seen as a mark of social stability. This high
culture, the one we know from the literati's records, intellectual and aesthetic, was given full play only in times of social peace, when dynasty and bureaucracy (the "vanguard
of the literati") seemed in reasonably good working order.
But, one must remember, the stability of traditional
Chinese society was not the stability of perpetual peace but
the stability of a cycle of breakdown and reconstitution
(with progressive articulation, through Sung, of the stabiliz-
ing social institutions and intellectual formulations that
had been adumbrated in Ch'in and Han times, the first
great empire period). And just as it was characteristic of the
bureaucratic society both to cohere and to break down, so it
was characteristic of Confucianism and Taoism both to be
linked and to be pulled apart.

Harmony between Taoism and Confucianism was the intellectual reflection of social peace. Tension between
Taoism and Confucianism was the intellectual reflection of
social strain. Taoism (or later, Buddhism or Christianity)
came to be advocated as explicitly anti-Confucian in the
breakdown phase of the cycle. In that phase, when Confucianism itself became more *symbolic* than *significant* (i.e.,
more the mark of officials' privilege than the ethical content
of officials' good example), Taoism became a symbol of
defection from the gentry-literati-official powerholders in
the Confucian state.

We shall defer analysis of Confucianism and Taoism as
symbolic opposites until our discussion of Han social history
brings us to the breakdown phase in this first great turn of
the cycle. It was then that Taoism, in different manifestations ("neo-Taoism" for the first, "popular" or "religious

Taoism" for the second) became a protest expression of escapist intelligentsia and rebellious peasantry. We may then grasp the full complexity of the relationship of Confucianism and Taoism. In the ambivalence of this intellectual relationship — part harmony and correlation, part rivalry and dissociation — we may see an illumination of Chinese society, with its centripetal tendency to social unity and order and its centrifugal tendency to social strain and breakdown.

Background

The "Yellow Turbans" and the End of the First Great Dynastic Period: the Descent into Disunity

As during the period of the Warring States, economic progress and sociopolitical disintegration went hand in hand during the time of the Later (or Eastern) Han. Cities continued to develop. New technological devices were introduced. Agricultural production increased. New sources of wealth were tapped. Yet, as in so many other societies (one might cite pre-1914 Russia as an example), the accumulation of wealth benefited only a part of society, and the phenomenon of rapid socioeconomic mobility for some had disruptive consequences for others. The appearance of a "kulak" (rich peasant) class meant ruin for less capable peasants. Continuing attacks by nomads on the frontiers made for permanent instability among the agricultural population of the border regions. The lure of new lands in south China started an internal migration. The growing ineffectiveness of the state in exercising control led to the rise of local elites — the sources of aristocracies in the coming "Six Dynasties" period. Economic exploitation became fiercer, and village solidarity was threatened. The growing power of the local elites and the disintegration of social stability would ultimately topple the increasingly brittle structure of the Han state. But before the final disaster occurred, the signs of collapse became visible in revolt and rebellion.

If economic progress itself began to eat at the bonds of the basic social structure, frequent natural disasters, of a sort that has afflicted China to this day, often snapped the bonds entirely. Natural disaster meant immediate hunger, and hunger forced peasants to leave their villages and wander in search of food. Chinese sources, from Han times on, recount widespread instances of *liu-wang*, wandering men scouring distant regions for work and food. It is significant that the English language has no single word for this phenomenon, but it exists in Russian — *brodiazhestvo* — and was widely used in the period before 1914. One might think that the power of the Chinese family system, a system tending to root individuals to their ancestral homes, would have prevented emigration, no matter how terrible the human conditions. Yet, already in Han times the nuclear family was the unit of Chinese family life, and the great family system, so often highly praised by Confucian scholars, hardly reached lower than the rural elite. Later Chinese stories repeatedly tell of poor men leaving their families to seek work, returning only decades later, often to find little left of their original family. As the Han sources frequently mention *liu-wang*, other words, inspired by these phenomena, also appear: "bandits," "pirates," "robbers." From 107 A.D. on, these terms appear with increasing frequency in the sources. In their isolation and poverty, these "wanderers" began to form bands that had no recourse but to prey on society for a livelihood.

After 137 A.D., the sources begin to report something new: peasant revolts with an ideological element. This element invariably takes a religious form, not a Confucian one (with Confucianism's emphasis on rationality and conservatism) but "Taoist," in a loose sense of the word, with a characteristic irrationality and a menacing social radicalism. It is these new religious beliefs that form the values, the ideology, from which disparate and motley bandit groups forge a new organization. A new term appears in the sources: *yao-tsei*, "magic bandits." One must remember that history is generally written by the victors, and they rarely have much comprehension of the motivations of the vanquished. To the Confucian historians and officials of the time and of later generations, these bandits were stirring up the dark world of magic, the terrible forces of superstition, which Confucian rationality sought to tame in man. As a famous Sung Confucian history (twelfth century) ingenuously put it: "They abandoned their homes, they sold their property, and in streams came to him. . . . The prefects and subprefects did not understand their ideas."

In a much later age, the time of the T'ai-p'ing (Taiping) Rebellion, 1850–1864, a reading of government (Ch'ing dynasty) and Taiping literature on similar themes reveals the spiritual gap that separated the two sides. The incomprehension of the supporters of the status quo, however, had another element in it: fear. The peasant rebellions were not only local attacks on rich men and government officials, but began to take on maximal political aims. With increasing frequency, the leaders of the rebellions began to call themselves "emperor." The universalistic fantasies of religion soon led to the universalistic fantasies of politics. The conquest of total power became the aim of the rebels, who remembered only too well how the Han themselves had risen to supremacy.

A contemporary Chinese Communist historian speaks of the "religious faith and religious church organization (of these rebels) which made it possible to organize scattered groups of peasants" — the sort of feat that the Communists have repeatedly claimed as their own. During the Later Han era there were two main religiosocial groups. One called itself "The Way of Great Peace"; the other was known as "The Way of the Five Pecks of Rice." The term "Yellow Turbans" was applied to the former by their Han opponents, from the characteristic headgear that marked them (just as the term, "Long-haired bandits", was applied to the nineteenth-century Taipings by their Ch'ing enemies). There seems to have been an element of chiliastic fantasy in the ideology of the Yellow Turbans. Violence would sweep away the evils of contemporary society, and total triumph would bring with it the millennium of the "great peace." This curious and contradictory association of total violence with total peace was to be seen again in Chinese history, and indeed it was a characteristic of apocalyptic religious movements in medieval Europe.

The Yellow Turbans arose sometime during the reign of Shun-ti (126–144 A.D.). An item in one of the biographies of Han leaders mentions the forwarding to the court of "170 volumes of divine books that Commander Yü Chi captured at the headwaters of the Ch'ü-yang River . . . they were called 'the books of pure guidance of the Great Peace.' They were written in the manner of the Yin-yang and Five-Elements schools, and had many words of sorceresses and sorcerers. The authorities reported that [the books] forwarded to the Court by [Prince] Ch'ung were magical lies and not canonical. Therefore, they were confiscated." Later, Chang Chüeh would have many of these same books.

Chang Chüeh was the greatest leader of the Yellow Turbans, not only a great rebel but their thaumaturge. The location where these books were captured, at the headwaters of a river, shows that these rebels had ensconced themselves in remote fastnesses, mountain retreats, like modern guerrillas. The imputation of magic reveals the Han's incomprehension of the nature of the enemy they were beginning to contend with.

If our knowledge of the Yellow Turbans is limited, that of "The Way of the Five Pecks of Rice" is even more so. The name probably derives from the practice of followers' giving five pecks of rice to their leaders. They arose in central China, in Szechwan, near modern Chungking, a different area from that of the Yellow Turbans.

The Yellow Turbans were led by three brothers, Chang Chüeh, Chang Pao, and Chang Liang. The "Five Pecks" were led by three men, Chang Ling, Chang Heng, and Chang Lu, directly descended from a common ancestor. The surname Chang, though fairly common in China, would continue to have a curious association with Taoism through the centuries. Both major groups of rebels, as well as minor ones, emphasized faith healing. An item in one of the later sources describes the procedure:

Among the followers of *T'ai-p'ing-tao* [The Way of the Great Peace], the leader clasps a nine-jointed staff as a prayer wand. He calls upon the sick man to prostrate himself and think about his faults. Then with the wand he gives him water to drink. If as the days go by the sickness gets better, it is said: he believes in the Way. If the sickness gets worse, then it is said: he does not believe in the Way. . . . The methods of [the "Five Peck" sect] are on the whole similar to those of Chang Chüeh, but they emphasize even more the carrying out of quiescence in a room, with the sick man made to sit in the center and meditate on his faults. They also have someone act as a "depraved leader" to sacrifice wine. The sacrificial leader makes them learn the 5000 words of Lao-tzu. . . . They are known as "depraved leaders" or as "devil's clerks"; mostly they pray for the sick man. The way they pray is like this: they write down the name of the sick man, and speak of the sins he has committed. They make three copies. One is presented to Heaven, and placed on top of a mountain. One is buried in the earth. The third is immersed in a river. These are called the hand writings of the three officials. They always make the sick man offer five pecks of rice from his family, and that is why they are called the "Five Pecks of Rice leaders."

Aside from healing, these rebels had definite social policies. Chang Lu, who succeeded his father, Chang Heng, in preaching the "Five Peck" doctrine in central China, established public buildings in which grain and meat were stored. The faithful could stay overnight in these buildings during their travels, and be fed. We may assume that the Yellow Turbans developed similar practices.

Chang Chüeh, the leader of the Yellow Turbans, came from southwest Hopei. He called himself "the good doctor of great wisdom." Within ten years he had gathered together several hundreds of thousands of followers. Though concentrated in eastern China, his activities ranged far to the south and west, finding adherents particularly among the peasantry. They were well organized, into 36 "squares," — "large squares" consisting of 10,000 individuals, and "small squares" of 6000–7000 — each led by a deputy "doctor." He preached not only enmity to the Han dynasty but its imminent demise: "The blue heaven has died, the yellow heaven shall arise!" Underground agents wrote the characters *chiatzu* of the sexagenary cycle, the year 184 A.D., on the doors of

officials. 184 was to be the year of decision, and to this end
Ma Yüan-i, one of the "great square" leaders, went secretly
to Loyang, the capital, where he made contact with certain
Court eunuchs, high in official favor. The fifth day of the
third moon had been fixed for a general uprising in Loyang
and surrounding regions. But traitors within the movement
had betrayed the plans of the rebels to the Court.

Ma Yüan-i was captured and executed; and Chang
Chüeh, as soon as he was informed of this, ordered the rising immediately. The peasant rebels wound yellow turbans
around their heads (so that the yellow heaven would recognize them for its own), and burst out with the cry: "Burn
the official residences, loot the towns!" A wave of panic
gripped officialdom. Fortifications were thrown up around
Loyang. Troops were sent out to battle the hordes of rebels.
All over the countryside wealthy landowners organized their
own armies to defend themselves. Political strife at the Han
court that had given rise to cliques and factions was forgotten in the face of the common danger.

As almost seventeen centuries later during the great Taiping Rebellion, great and fateful names would emerge from
the leaders of the counter-rebellion: Tung Cho, Ts'ao
Ts'ao, Liu Pei. Han bureaucracy had failed to keep the
state structure together, and the bitterness of Court squab-
bles had emasculated the monarchy. The only recourse was
to turn to men of strength, men capable of organizing and
leading armies. The rebellion was crushed, but the seeds of
the final Han tragedy had been sown.

The rebellion spread far beyond Loyang. Though brave
and fanatical in battle, the rebels were no match for the tal-
ented generals who opposed them, and this, together with
the opposition of the local gentry, doomed the Yellow Turbans. Within a year the rebellion had been virtually
crushed, with hundreds of thousands of peasant casualties.
Sporadic revolts continued to break out, notably in Chang
Chüeh's native Hopei, but the rebellion's heart had ceased
to beat.

Yet, the revolt had shaken the foundations of the Later
Han power. The local gentry, thrown on their own resources, had recognized their power and enhanced it. They
removed themselves more and more from the control of the

Court. When Tung Cho, whose power base was in the west, seized control of Loyang, the stronger gentry families and local potentates of central China broke away almost completely from the vanishing central government. The son of Ts'ao Ts'ao, Ts'ao P'ei, in describing the struggle against Tung Cho, commented despairingly on the situation: "The great and the powerful, rich men and strong families storm about like swarms of clouds, going through thousands of miles. . . . The great control whole provinces and countries. The middling ones gather in cities and towns. The smallest have accumulated great lands." After 190 A.D., though the Han still existed in name (until 220 A.D.), actual control was in the hands of the great local leaders — Yüan Shao, Yüan Shu, Ts'ao Ts'ao, Liu Pei, Sun Ts'e, and others. A new period in Chinese history had begun.

Reading

Welch, Holmes, *The Parting of the Way: Lao Tzu and the Taoist Movement* (Boston: Beacon Press, 1966). Paperback (original edition 1957).

Implications

Intellectual Implications of Social Stability: (b) Confucianism and Taoism as Symbolic Opposites

TAOISM AND SOCIAL STRAIN IN CHINESE SOCIETY

In accounts of dynastic crises one may read such statements as this: "Crowds of the starving were to be seen wandering about the country and invoking the Taoist deities." What is the meaning of this juxtaposition of "starving" with

"Taoist"? What has Taoism, which must be discussed in categories of philosophical abstraction, to do with actual people in a social situation? And further what is the meaning of this injection of a religious note, this mention of Taoist *deities*? How is Taoism as a philosophy linked with Taoism as a religion (both are called Taoism, after all), and how are the two at the same time distinguished from each other? Does this distinction between philosophy and cult have something to do with the Taoist connection with the socially submerged or uprooted?

To understand the specifically Taoist nature of the Yellow Turban revolt of mainly illiterate peasants against a Confucian-official regime, it would be well to reflect again on the intellectual distinction between Taoism and Confucianism. Recapitulation can be made in most pithy fashion by our referring once more to their different conceptions of knowledge. Taoism insisted that to understand the meaning or significance of a thing one must become the thing, harmonize one's consciousness with it and reach a mental attitude which brings knowledge without that Confucian activity, intellectual deliberation. Subjective and objective become identical. As it says in *Chuang Tzu*: "to place oneself in subjective relation with externals, without consciousness of their objectivity — this is Tao." (Cf. T. S. Eliot, "The Dry Salvages": ". . . music heard so deeply that it is not heard at all, but you are the music/While the music lasts . . ."). In the famous fifth-century A.D. painters' canon, the "six principles" of Hsieh Ho, the elliptical first principle (*ch'i-yün sheng-tung*, "spirit-consonance, life-movement") was always taken in a Taoist sense. The painter is to seize on (not learn about) those external features best fitted to convey the inner life, *ch'i*, spirit. He is, as it were, tuned in on the *tao*, at one with his subject, not striving in the slow way of acquiring knowledge, piling up sense perceptions from the outside.

Taoist intuitiveness, then, was a philosophical alternative to Confucian intellectuality, but as a philosophy, in its implications for art and life, it was fundamentally congenial to Confucianists. It animated high art and high philosophy, that is, high culture or civilization, and Confucianists, after all, were devoted to civilization. However, a Taoist *religion* as an alternative to Confucianism was not congenial to Confucian literati, but contemptible. The religión became associated with the great mass of nongentry.

It was never Taoism that caused peasants to rise in revolt. Civil wars in China were never at bottom religious wars, with Taoists trying to smash Confucianism out of religious hostility to doctrine. Rather, peasants rose in revolt because of social pressures, when the ideal Confucian social harmony was too outrageously a fiction; and the popular, religious Taoism became a sign — like the yellow turbans themselves — of a peasant avowal of alienation from the ruling order which was officially Confucian. A well-fed official might write a philosophically Taoist poem, as relief from the Confucian cares of office. But a starving peasant might invoke the Taoist deities, and set out to kill the Confucian official.

FROM TAOIST PHILOSOPHY TO TAOIST RELIGION: INTELLECTUAL DERIVATION

This distinction between Taoisms was expressed in Han times by identification of two Taoist schools:

Lao-Chuang (Lao Tzu and Chuang Tzu), which denied the importance of death.

Huang-Lao (Huang Ti [the Yellow Emperor] and Lao Tzu), which sought the elixir of life. (It is possible however, that the Huang Ti–Lao Tzu definition of the term is only a post-Han scholarly assumption, while in Han times the compound referred to a favorite Taoist deity of the Yellow Turbans, Huang-lao Chün.)*

It is in this change of emphasis — from the attempt to banish *consciousness* of death, to the attempt to banish death by reaching physical immortality — that we see the popularization of Taoism. *Both* are Taoism (note that the *Lao* element is common to both), both are concerned with the meaning of life and death. But one was trying, by mystic insight, to transcend man's limitations, while the other was trying, by magic and protoscience, not to change man's understanding of what life is, but to perpetuate and ameliorate precisely this life he knows.

* *Huang-lao* had another meaning as well, in Han times; it referred to a political philosophy of *laisser-faire*.

The philosophical Taoist hermit (whom we know from painting and the other arts cultivated by Confucianists) simply vanishes from society to become one with nature, to *lose himself* in nature — that is, not to get lost physically, so that other people cannot find his body, but to lose *consciousness of himself* (or, the same thing, to lose consciousness of the "otherness" of things). But in popular Taoism the hermit becomes an "immortal" — that is, one who does not "lose himself" (a mental operation) but does precisely the reverse, physically perpetuating himself. In philosophical Taoism, again, the dragon is the symbol of Tao, in its sense of cosmic all-pervasive force which man can never master: see the "dragon scroll" (Boston Museum of Fine Arts) by Ch'en Jung, thirteenth-century Taoist painter, in which the dragons move magnificently through the clouds and are never entirely seen (Lao-tzu: "The way that can be known is not the eternal way" — *Tao k'o tao fei ch'ang tao*). But in popular Taoism the dragon, still the symbol of the Tao, is emphasized as the "male principle," the guarantor of physical potency, the expression of a drive toward life and vitality that is an extension of the life man knows.

It is, then, an emphasis on the *physical* that characterizes popular Taoism, and its relation to philosophical Taoism can be described, in one sense, as a physical interpretation (or mis-interpretation) of intellectual concepts. For example, in one of the main subdivisions of the Yellow Turbans there was a class of men who commanded troops and at the same time taught religion. They were supposed to know by heart the *Tao te ching* (which shows their direct line to philosophy), but the latter became — without any modification of text, just by an accompanying explanation — an exposition of Yellow Turban religious practices, with the most abstract passages allegorized in amazing physical fashion.

In sum, then: The aim of philosophical Taoism was mystic union with eternal Tao, the first principle of all things, eternal, impersonal, immanent in all. But Taoists in general were not on this peak, and potentialities for derivative vulgarization were seen early. Chuang Tzu records the arrival among his disciples of a man who asked of him "the process of preserving life, and nothing else." This was the aim of most Taoists in the religious organizations. Another late work (ca. 300 A.D., though purporting to be early), *Lieh Tzu* shows what could be derived from this Taoism, for the *Lieh Tzu* was full of stories of magic and marvels. Finally, in popular Taoism, all sorts of dietetic, respiratory, magical, and alchemical practices abounded.

There were breathing exercises to induce trance. There developed ideas of "natural foods," and sexual acts as sympathetic magic, to instill strength. Above all there was alchemy, the search for ways to transform elements of matter, in hopes of finding an elixir of life. This included such efforts as to arrive at the *essence* of gold, that is, to separate its immanent *tao* from dross so as to get a potable form of underlying reality. And there was another sort of alchemy, to the same end: the effort to produce allegedly life-preserving substances like jade and cinnabar artificially, to release them from the inhibiting "impurities" of their natural state. From here it was not far to secular goals like those of western alchemy and protochemistry, such as efforts to produce gold from baser metals. That is how the affinities of science in China came to be mainly popular-Taoist. It was entirely consistent of Confucianism, which looked with such scorn and fearful incomprehension on Taoist religious "enthusiasm," to be a drag on science as well.

LITERATI-ESCAPIST TAOISM

Works on alchemy and the like were written down, and we must recognize the existence of a literati fringe in popular Taoism. But there was a more prominent association of literati with a Taoist divergence from Confucian values; there was an upper-class defection from Confucianism, different in substance from lower-class rebellion, but similarly comprehensible as a response to the seeming collapse of Confucian society with the decline and fall of Han. Highly speculative commentaries on the *Book of Changes*, the *Lao Tzu*, and the *Chuang Tzu* formed the core of the "dark learning," with its orientation to "emptiness and nonbeing" instead of to social and political thought. The main intellectual movement of the third century A.D. was quite different in tone from the Yellow Turban movement, but it, too, was an anti-Confucianist Taoism (though nominally it kept

Confucius — a most un-"Confucian" Confucius — as the su-persage).

This was the movement called *ch'ing-t'an*, "pure talk," an expression of pessimism and disillusion with the world of political society. Hedonism — skepticism about duty, cere-mony, and Confucian sobriety — were the hallmarks. The most famous group related to "pure-talk" was "The Seven Sages of the Bamboo Grove," flourishing ca. 260 A.D., and Chinese tradition came to be somewhat ambivalent about it. To some extent, the "Seven Sages" achieved the philosophi-cal-correlative acceptance, as ideal Taoists in the Confu-cian-syncretic sense; but to some extent, too, they were stig-matized as enemies of culture.

As philosophically acceptable they formed part of a famil-iar art motif, in which, disposed informally under a bam-boo, the venerables variously playing chess, writing poetry, playing and listening to the lute, and drinking a cup of wine, they symbolized abstraction from the world of social cares. This suggested the euphoria of harmony with Tao, and it represents a later Confucian domestication of these figures by putting them into a philosophical Taoist setting congenial to Confucianists. But there was a different Confu-cian interpretation in their own times and soon after. There is a letter extant, and a bitter Confucian comment thereon, in which one of the seven broke off relations with a high of-ficial who had recommended him as his own successor. The sage in question (perhaps dissembling more personal rea-sons) declared that he could not bring himself to join the vulgar crowd of officials — more than that, he criticized the traditional founders of the Shang and Chou dynasties, whom Confucianists had always acclaimed as virtuous rulers, mod-els for all generations to come. The earlier founders of "pure talk" had set the precedent for such disparagement of Confucian society, and they were contemptuously belabored by later Confucianists as symbols of excess. A fourth-century scholar blamed the post-Han debacle of Chinese civilization on them, alleging that their crimes were worse than those of the last kings of Hsia and Shang, the two greatest villains in the Confucian reading of history. A situation in which Chinese scholars surrendered themselves to drink, neglected to mourn for parents, and went naked (these were all accusations of Confucian traducers of "pure talk") vividly suggested collapse of the Confucian moral structure.

Naturally, from the Confucian point of view which has morality (Confucian-established) as the governor of history, this kind of literati defection from Confucianism was the cause of disorder in Chinese society. From the point of view of nonmoralistic moderns (diverging from Confucian historical thinking here as it does in the case of Chinese origins), literati Taoism of this sort seems less a cause of disorder than a response to it. Like the religious Taoism of the popular masses, it was a Taoism set in opposition to Confucianism when the state structure — a Confucian structure — fell into decay. Here, of course, was not the active social opposition exemplified in peasant cults; the opposition now was not that of seceding peasants but of deserting intellectuals, trying not to reverse prevailing social conditions but rather to escape them. In both cases, peasant and literati, a reaction to Confucian social collapse was represented in Taoist terms. But the Taoism itself varied with the social interest involved.

Thus, we may see Taoism and Confucianism as symbolic opposites as well as philosophical correlatives. For ideas generally are both *significant* (have meaning, in an abstract philosophical sense) and *symbolic* (represent, in relation to one another, the relation of social groups which may respectively espouse them). In Chinese history Confucian belief and mastery of Confucian texts were not just authentic or distorted expressions of what Confucius meant (i.e., philosophical), but also a mark of social status and a key to social power. And Taoism (or, later, Buddhism), just so far as it was a philosophical rival of Confucianism, could be adopted (and adapted) as a symbol of social hostility to Confucianists who ruled in a Confucian state.

This social hostility proved regularly to be of a rebellious, not a revolutionary type; social strains recurrently became unbearable, but social uprisings were not the agencies to change the quality of imperial-bureaucratic society. And perhaps this scope for rebellion with no scope for revolution was itself symbolized in the ambivalent relationship of Confucianism with Taoism (and Buddhism, as we shall see): a relationship of rivalry, but of *appeasable* rivalry, with syncretisms ultimately possible. Confucianism and Taoism (and Confucianism and Buddhism) could be united in the gentry's creed. And the gentry — however threatened, as it sometimes was, by exponents of a radically independent Taoism or Buddhism, and however structurally modified — was always, down to modern times, reconstituted.

A Note on Bibliography

This work is meant to be a practical tool for the study of history, not an encyclopedic reference book. Accordingly, as supplementary reading for individual topics, we append to the background section titles bearing on the subject or on major segments of it. The titles (with few exceptions) are those of readily available books in English — paperback, wherever possible — so that they may be easily purchased as the core of a working library. For reference bibliographies, in order of increasing comprehensiveness, we call attention to the following:

Hucker, Charles O., *Chinese History: A Bibliographic Review* (Washington, D.C.: Service Center for Teachers of History, American Historical Association, 1958).

Hucker, Charles O., *China: A Critical Bibliography* (Tucson: University of Arizona Press, 1962).

Yuan Tung-li, *China in Western Literature: A Continuation of Cordier's Bibliotheca Sinica* (New Haven: Far Eastern Publications, Yale University, 1958).

For bibliography (articles as well as books) since the dates of these publications, consult the annual bibliographical supplements of *The Journal of Asian Studies* (formerly *The Far Eastern Quarterly*, whose annual bibliographical supplement was first published in 1947).

Following are important volumes of (a) collected articles, by one author or by several; (b) anthologies of translated source materials; and (c) general histories of specific aspects of Chinese civilization. These may be read to great advantage in conjunction with various topics throughout the present volume.

(a) Balazs, Etienne, *Chinese Civilization and Bureaucracy* (New Haven and London: Yale University Press, 1967). Paperback (original edition 1964).

Bishop, John L., ed., *Studies of Governmental Institutions in Chinese History* (Cambridge, Mass.: Harvard University Press, 1968). Paperback.

Yang Lien-sheng, *Studies in Chinese Institutional History* (Cambridge, Mass.: Harvard University Press, 1961).

(b) Birch, Cyril, ed., *Anthology of Chinese Literature: Vol. I, from early times to the 14th century* (New York: Grove Press, 1967). Paperback (original edition 1965).

de Bary, W. T., *et al.*, ed., *Sources of Chinese Tradition* (New York and London: Columbia University Press, 1964). Paperback, 2 vols. (originally published in one vol., 1960).

(c) Fung Yu-lan (translated and adapted by Derk Bodde), *A Short History of Chinese Philosophy* (New York: Free Press, 1966). Paperback (original edition 1948).

Hightower, James R., *Topics in Chinese Literature: Outlines and Bibliographies*, revised edition (Cambridge, Mass.: Harvard University Press, 1953).

Needham, Joseph, *Science and Civilization in China*, 7 vols. projected (Cambridge: Cambridge University Press, 1954 *et seq.*). See I, pp. 55–72, for the best brief description of the geographical setting.

Sullivan, Michael, *A Short History of Chinese Art* (Berkeley and Los Angeles: University of California Press, 1967). Paperback.

Yang Lien-sheng, *Money and Credit in China: A Short History* (Cambridge, Mass.: Harvard University Press, 1952).

Index

Achilles, 54

Aeneas, 54

Agriculture, 10, 11, 18, 23, 24, 27, 28, 29, 30, 33, 61, 68, 119

Alchemy, 129

An-yang, 10, 11, 13, 16, 21, 22, 23, 27, 30

Analects, (*Lun-yü*), 48, 49, 50, 54, 58

Anarchist, anarchism, 60, 63, 65, 113

Ancestor worship, 20, 21, 32

Anhwei, 9

Arab, 36

Aristocracy, 39, 40, 62, 67, 68, 76, 81, 86, 119

Aristotle, 114

Armies, 22, 31, 33, 67, 80

Art, 105, 111, 112, 113, 126, 128, 130

Artisans, 22

Assimilation, 106, 107

Assyria, 36

Austria, 39

Authority, 38, 39, 58, 72, 76, 80, 81, 82, 87, 88

Autocracy, 62

Babylonia, 114

Bandits, 120

Barbarians, 66, 69, 104 ff., 113, 114, 115

Beneficium, 37

Bielenstein, Hans, 98n

Bloch, Marc, 38, 40

Bodde, Derk, 5n, 34n, 84n

Book of Changes (*I-ching*), 43, 83, 129

Book of Documents (*Shu-ching*), 5, 15, 29, 44, 53, 83, 87

Book of Lord Shang (*Shang Chün shu*), 60, 61

Book of Songs (or *Odes*) (*Shih-ching*), 15, 20, 44, 52, 53, 83

Book of Rites (*Li-chi*), 44, 45, 57, 83

Books, 71, 83, 90

Bourgeoisie, 99

Bronzes, 13

Buddhism, 62, 65, 117, 131, 132

Bureaucracy, 19, 20, 32, 39, 67, 68, 73, 74, 76, 77, 80, 82, 83, 84 ff., 93, 98 ff., 117, 131

Canton, 107

Capital, 16, 17, 22, 24, 30, 31, 33, 98 ff.

Capitalism, 35, 73, 74, 75, 76, 77, 78

Carolingian, 37, 39

Central Asia, 16, 24, 29, 97, 108

Central Plain, 8

Ch'ang-an, 81, 108

Chang Ch'ien, 108

Chang Chüeh, 122, 123, 124

Chang Hen, 122, 123

Chang Kwang-chih, 11n, 24n

Chang Liang, 122

Chang Ling, 122

Chang Lu, 122, 123

Chang Pao, 122

Ch'ang-sha, 82

Change, 48, 49. *See also*: Innovation

Chao, 82

Chao Kao, 81

Charisma, 19

Ch'en Jung, 128

Ch'eng Wang, 30

Chi, 67

Ch'i, 11, 16

Ch'i (state of), 69

Chia I, 87

Ch'iang, 17, 23, 28. *See also* Tibetans

Chiang-yüan, 28

Chieh, 12

Chih ("humane wisdom"), 57

Chiliastic fantasies, 121

135

INDEX

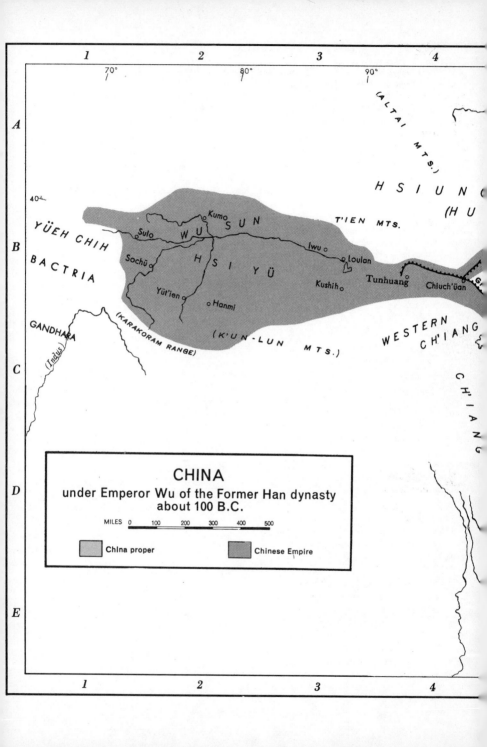

CHINA
under Emperor Wu of the Former Han dynasty
about 100 B.C.

MILES 0 100 200 300 400 500

China proper   Chinese Empire